Essential
Egypt

by Sylvie Franquet & Anthony Sattin

Above: *brightly coloured wall-paintings in Gurna illustrate the family's daily life and pilgrimage to Mecca*

PASSPORT BOOKS
NTC/Contemporary Publishing Group

Egyptian fellaheen (farmers) still preserve many of the traditions inherited from their ancestors

Front cover: felucca *at Aswan; man on a camel; relief at Saqqara*

Back cover: *pomegranates*

This edition first published in 2000 by Passport Books, a division of NTC/ Contemporary Publishing Group, Inc., 4255 West Touhy Avenue, Lincolnwood (Chicago), Illinois 60712–1975 U.S.A.

Reprinted December 2000
Copyright © Automobile Association Developments Ltd 2000
Maps © Automobile Association Developments Ltd 2000

The contents of this publication are believed correct at the time of printing. Nevertheless, the publishers cannot accept responsibility for errors or omissions, nor for changes in details given. We are always grateful to readers who let us know of any errors or omissions they come across, and future printings will be updated accordingly.

Published by Passport Books in conjunction with The Automobile Association of Great Britain.

Written by Sylvie Franquet & Anthony Sattin

Library of Congress Catalog Card Number: on file
ISBN 0-658-00633-9

Colour separation: Chroma Graphics (Overseas) Pte Ltd, Singapore

Printed and bound in Italy by Printer Trento srl

Contents

About this Book

Essential *Egypt* is divided into five sections to cover the most important aspects of your visit to Egypt.

Viewing Egypt pages 5–14
An introduction to Egypt by the authors.
  Egypt's Features
  Essence of Egypt
  The Shaping of Egypt
  Peace and Quiet
  Egypt's Famous

Top Ten pages 15–26
The author's choice of the Top Ten places to see in Egypt, listed in alphabetical order, each with practical information.

What to See pages 27–90
The five main areas of Egypt, each with its own brief introduction and an alphabetical listing of the main attractions.
  Practical information
  Snippets of 'Did you know…' information
  1 suggested boat trip
  2 suggested walks
  3 features

Where To... pages 91–116
Detailed listings of the best places to eat, stay, shop, take the children and be entertained.

Practical Matters pages 117–24
A highly visual section containing essential travel information.

Maps
All map references are to the individual maps found in the What to See section of this guide.
For example, Karnak has the reference
🕇 29D3 – indicating the page on which the map is located and the grid square in which the site is to be found. A list of the maps that have been used in this travel guide can be found in the index.

Prices
Where appropriate, an indication of the cost of an establishment is given by **£** signs:

£££ denotes higher prices, **££** denotes average prices, while **£** denotes lower charges.

Star Ratings
Most of the places described in this book have been given a separate rating:
😀😀😀 Do not miss
😀😀 Highly recommended
😀 Worth seeing

Viewing
Egypt

Above: *a bright yellow mosque in the Nile Delta*
Below: *a farmer uses age-old farming methods*

The Authors' Egypt

Change of Direction
The usual route for tourists in the past was to arrive in Cairo and then travel up the Nile to Luxor, and then on to Aswan. However, many people now head for the Red Sea coast or Sinai and make excursions to see the antiquities in Luxor, while more adventurous visitors are travelling further south along the Red Sea towards Sudan or making trips into the Western Desert. However, before setting off independently bear in mind that Egypt is still prone to security alerts (► 122, Personal Safety).

There is always space for a market in Egypt, even within a busy gate to Cairo's old city

Sylvie and I were first drawn to Egypt for very different reasons. For me it was the chance to visit some of the most famous and rewarding relics of mankind's past and to soak up what I was assured was guaranteed sunshine (they were wrong – it also rains occasionally!). Sylvie first went to Cairo to continue her Arabic studies and to take in the atmosphere of the Arab world's largest and most significant city.

Egypt has it all, we discovered. With a long history behind it an uncertain future ahead, it is a country in flux. You see the signs everywhere, from satellite dishes in villages to four-wheel drive cars in the desert. A considerable part of the heavy debt burden that held Egypt back in the 1980s was written off after its help in the Gulf War, and US aid and the end of restrictions on moving money have helped the economy. The appearance of prosperity is conspicuous and you get used to seeing new cars and mobile phones. But whatever happens, there are two things that will never change and, in a way, these are the things that kept us in the country. One is Egypt's position at the crossroads between Africa, Arabia, Asia and Europe. The other is the influence of the past. After 2000 years of foreign rule and influence, Egyptians have preserved something of both their physical and spiritual heritage. That unique heritage is what draws us – and you – to see them and their country.

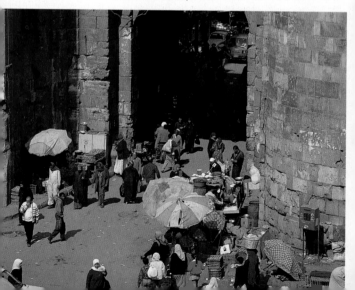

Egypt's Features

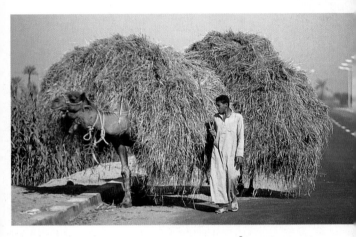

Egyptians

Egypt's 64 million inhabitants are a young community (more than a third are under 15), some 90 per cent of whom are Muslims, the majority of the rest being Coptic Christians, with a small population of Jews and Christian denominations. Population movements have added to the racial characteristics of ancient Egyptians, exemplified in tomb paintings. Greeks and other Europeans in the north, the darker-skinned, distinctive features of Nubians in the south and the Semitic Arabs and Bedouins from the deserts to east and west have all had a marked influence.

The Land

Ancient Egypt was divided into red land (desert) and black land (valley and delta). More than 97 per cent of Egypt's approximately 1 million sq km is desert, much of it low-lying, but also containing mountains, the highest being Gebel Katarina in Sinai (2,228m). The majority of the population lives on 33,000sq km of flat, fertile land irrigated by the Nile, which is intensively farmed.

Economy

Oil production, Suez Canal revenues, tourism and money sent home by Egyptian workers abroad account for the majority of foreign currency earnings. Some 35 per cent of Egyptians work in agriculture, 17 per cent of the workforce is unemployed, 10 per cent of all jobs rely on tourism and more than 75 per cent of Egyptians survive on an annual family income of not more than US$600 (1993 figures).

Above: *many Egyptians still live off the land*
Below: *children are considered to be God's blessing*

Egyptians Abroad
Until the Gulf crisis of 1990–1, more than a million Egyptians worked in the Gulf. The money they sent home was crucial to the government and to their families. Their return to Egypt during the war created great social instability, but in recent years many have resumed work in the Gulf.

Essence of Egypt

Egypt boasts three of the greatest cities the world has known: pharaonic Thebes (Luxor), so important that the Egyptians simply called it 'the City', ancient Alexandria, the great centre of classical learning, and Cairo, Africa's largest city and legendary 'mother of the world'. Three deserts make up the bulk of the country, forbidding places that still fill most Egyptians with horror. The Nile, the world's longest river, runs straight through it, making the land habitable. Finally there is that unique, rich and sensual light, which endows Egypt and its people with a touch of brilliance.

Very few tourists venture out into Egypt's deserts, which make up most of the country

THE **10** ESSENTIALS

If you only have a short time to visit Egypt, or would like to get a really complete picture of the country, here are some of the essentials :

• **See the pyramids at Giza** (➤ 17) – they are, quite simply, wonders of the ancient world.

• **Sail the Nile on a *felucca*** listening to the water against the prow, the boatman's song and the sound of villagers along the shore.

• **Explore the varied, mineral-rich desert** which makes up more than nine-tenths of the country.

• **Snorkel or dive in the Red Sea** (➤ 89) to glimpse the corals and colourful fish, but remember to leave them as you found them.

• **Watch a belly dancer** to understand the sensual rhythm of the people and to tune your ear to the sounds of Egypt's traditional music.

• **Visit a mosque** – all but two of Egypt's mosques are open to tourists. Some are among the country's most stunning buildings.

• **Bargain in the *souks*,** remembering to pit your wits – and humour – against the salesman's wiles and hospitality.

• **Marvel at the pharaohs' treasures** in museums throughout the country, but especially in Cairo's Egyptian Museum (➤ 23) and the Luxor Museum (➤ 68).

• **Linger over a mint tea** or *karkadeh* (hibiscus drink) in a café for a glimpse into Egyptian daily life.

• **Get lost wondering around Karnak** (➤ 20), the ultimate expression of the power, the skills, the sense of beauty and religious fervour of the ancient Egyptians.

Sailing on a felucca between Aswan's islands at the end of a hot afternoon is totally relaxing

Belly dancing, probably originally a fertility dance, still holds a central place in popular Egyptian culture

The Shaping of Egypt

Early Dynastic Period (3150–2686 BC)
*c*3050 BC
Egyptian civilisation begins, when the land is unified by a semi-mythical king, known as Narmer or Menes.

Old Kingdom (2686–2181 BC)
*c*2649 BC
King Djoser is buried in the world's first all-stone building, the Step Pyramid at Saqqara (➤ 48–9).

*c*2566 BC
The Pyramid age reaches its pinnacle with the building of the Great Pyramid for Pharaoh Cheops. More than 2.3 million blocks of stone are used.

Middle Kingdom (2040–1782 BC)
2040 BC
Mentuhotep I reunites Egypt after 250 years of chaos and political disorder.

New Kingdom (1570–1070 BC)
1350 BC
Amenhotep IV (Akhenaten) and Nefertiti, his wife, abandon the old gods to worship the sun god Aten at a new capital, Amarna. After Akhenaten's death in 1334 BC, his successor Tutankhaten restores the old order and the old god Amun, changing his own name to Tutankhamun.

1291–1278 BC
Seti I's reign is a high point in Egyptian art, as suggested by his temple at Abydos (➤ 16) and tomb in the Valley of the Kings (➤ 18). His son Ramses II boasted of his military prowess, but Egypt's empire is in decline.

331 BC
Alexander the Great founds Alexandria to bind ancient Egypt to the Mediterranean world. The dynasty created by his general, Ptolemy, rules Egypt until Cleopatra's suicide in 30 BC.

AD 45
According to legend, St Mark brings Christianity to Egypt. The Egyptian Coptic Church breaks links with other Christians in AD 451.

AD 641
Arab general Amr ibn el-As conquers Egypt, introduces Islam and sets up camp at Babylon (old Cairo). The city of Cairo isn't founded until AD 969, when Egypt is invaded by the Fatimids, a radical Shi'i sect from Tunisia.

1171–1193
The most famous of

Egypt's medieval rulers, Salah ad-Din (Saladin), a Kurd, liberates Syria and Jerusalem from the Crusaders and builds Cairo's Citadel (➤ 41).

1250–1517
The Mamelukes, Asian slave warriors, rule Egypt.

1517
Ottoman Turks invade and Egypt becomes a backwater in their empire. The route between Alexandria, Cairo and Suez becomes important as trade increases between Europe and the East. The British and French scheme to control it.

1798
Napoleon Bonaparte leads a French expedition of soldiers and scholars to Egypt and stimulates the study and removal of antiquities.

1805
An Albanian mercenary, Muhammad Ali, takes power and begins to modernise Egypt. His sons and grandson continue the work, culminating in the redesign of central Cairo and the opening of the Suez Canal in 1869.

1882
The bankruptcy of the government and an uprising in the Egyptian Army are the pretexts of a British invasion, but British troops remain for the next 74 years.

1952
King Farouk is overthrown by army officers including Gamel Abdel Nasser, who becomes President. When Nasser nationalises the Suez Canal in 1956, he sparks a conflict with Britain, France and Israel which leads to the final withdrawal of British troops.

1973
After several Arab-Israeli wars, both Egypt and Israel emerge from the

Ismail, Muhammad Ali's grandson, believed that with the Suez Canal, Egypt belonged to Europe

1973 conflict claiming victory. President Anwar Sadat negotiates the Camp David Peace Accord in 1979, which returns Sinai to Egypt.

1981
Sadat is assassinated and Hosni Mubarak becomes President.

1997
Sixty-eight people die in Luxor in a bloody series of demonstrations by Islamic fundamentalists against security forces and tourists.

11

Peace & Quiet

Urban Egypt can be a challenge to the senses and much of the coastline is crowded in summer, but there are no shortage of places where you can get away from it all.

The Nile

Some stretches of the river are busy with tourist boats, particularly in Cairo, Luxor and Aswan, but elsewhere the river is magnificent and makes a perfect retreat, particularly if you go on a silent *felucca* (➤ 78). Beyond the Aswan Dam, Lake Nasser is attracting a few more people in search of peace and quiet, but its vast expanse of water has hardly been disturbed (➤ 82–3). It is also home to massive fish (metre-long Nile perch are commonplace, while the largest recorded fish weighed some 200kg) and Nile crocodile, which haven't been seen north of the dam in living memory, but are reappearing in the lake.

Valley and Delta

You don't have to stray far from a road to discover peace in the countryside. Egyptian colours are straightforward – black earth, green crops and palm trees, blue sky and red sunsets (if you are lucky). As well as farmed animals, look out for egrets, hoopoes and scarab beetles, which, being the first creature to stir after the Nile floods subsided, symbolised resurrection to the ancient Egyptians.

El Faiyum

The colourful bee-eater overwinters in northern Africa; it favours hot, sheltered valleys with clumps of trees

Ancient Egyptians cut a canal from the Nile into a depression in the desert and created the Faiyum (➤ 46) and its lake, Birket Qarun. Only an hour's drive from Cairo, it is a rewarding retreat. Until early 20th century, Faiyum was a popular hunting ground and there are still duck and

many other wild birds, but as with the valley it is the peace of the farmland that is most refreshing.

The Deserts

Some 97 per cent of Egypt is desert and although the government has made great efforts to use it for mining, resettlement and, in the case of the new Toshka project, to green it, there is still plenty of empty space. Most of the Sinai peninsula (► 87) is desert, though of rocky plains and bare mountains rather than the sand dune variety. There is excellent birdwatching in spring and autumn along its western shore as migrating flocks navigate the Suez Canal. The Western or Libyan Desert, which includes the oases of Siwa, Bahariya, Kharga, Dakhla and Farafra (► 62–3), is becoming increasingly popular as a place of escape for Cairenes and their four-wheel drives, but still offers plenty of scope for peace. (Beware of going off-road alone in both the Sinai and northern Libyan Desert as mines left over from several wars are still claiming lives.)

The Red Sea mountains (► 90), between the Nile and the Red Sea, are mineral-rich and where the ancients cut gold, modern Egyptians extract phosphates and granite. Some of the earliest hermits came here for solitude and founded monasteries. In all the deserts, there is a chance of spotting jackals, snakes and scorpions.

Underwater

If you have already tried it then you will know that snorkelling, or better still, scuba diving is about as peaceful an activity as you can do. Exploring Egypt's spectacular coral reefs is a pleasure for experienced divers as well as novices. Serious divers are heading nearer the Sudanese border to escape the polluting effects of tourism developments. For recommended dive sites, ► 89.

Sinai's mountains look barren, but the wadis and canyons contains enough water to sustain interesting wildlife

The Western Desert Oases are surprisingly rich in wildlife, including insects – such as this dragonfly at the Siwa Oasis

1

Egypt's Famous

Akhenaton and Nefertiti

Akhenaton (14th century BC), who was born Amenhotep IV, abandoned the state cult of Amun, the priests and court at Thebes to found a new capital at Tell el-Amarna called Akhtetaten. He created his own religion, based on the worship of one god, the sun god Atar, and revolutionised the character of Egyptian art by introducing a much more realistic style. Nefertiti, his wife, stands as an ideal of ancient beauty.

Cleopatra had a son called Caesarion – by popular belief the child of Julius Caesar – and three more children by Mark Anthony

Tutankhamun

Akhenaton's only son, the nine year old boy-king Tutankhamun (died c1340 BC) returned the royal court to Luxor and reinstated Amun as state god after Akhenaton's heresy. He died in suspicious circumstances after a 9-year reign and lay almost undisturbed until Howard Carter opened his tomb in 1922.

Cleopatra

Cleopatra VI (69–30 BC) was banished from the throne by her younger brother Ptolemy XII, but she was reinstated in 47 BC when Julius Caesar came to Alexandria. Her name has become synonymous with seductive beauty – she had affairs with both Julius Caesar and Mark Anthony – but it is her suicide which sealed her fame, as she choose death rather than be taken in triumph to Rome. Look for her image at Dandara and in Alexandria's Graeco-Roman Museum.

Gamal Abdel Nasser

Nasser (1918–70) enjoyed success as one of the Free Officers who overthrew the monarchy and became Prime Minister and later the Republic's second president. He nationalised the Suez Canal and all manufacturing firms and financial institutions in order to finance the country's rapid industrialisation. Credited with building the Aswan Dam, he took responsibility for Egypt's defeat by Israel in the 1967 war. During his funeral in 1970 some 5 million people took to the streets.

President Hosni Mubarak
One of the inner circle of Free Officers who created the Arab Republic, Mubarak (1928–) has been president since the assassination of Anwar Sadat in 1981. Although he has been accused of lacking flair as a leader, more recently he has been admired for his steady handling of crises such as the Gulf War, fundamentalist violence and the great social changes currently sweeping Egypt.

Naguib Mahfouz

Naguib Mahfouz (born 1911), the grand old man of Egyptian letters, was awarded the Nobel Prize for Literature in 1988 for *The Cairo Trilogy*, set in the Cairo of his childhood in the early 1900s and told in the style of the great European novelists. Mahfouz is a traditionalist, and most of his novels are set in Islamic Cairo and Alexandria.

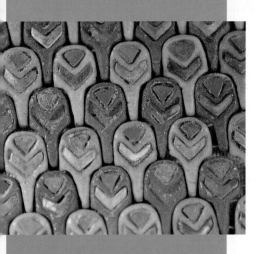

Top Ten

Above: *detail of fine enamelled jewellery found inside Tutankhamun's tomb*
Right: *wall-painting of ancient Egyptians making offerings to their gods*

1
Abydos

✝ 29D3

✉ El-Araba el-Madfuna, 10km south-west of el-Balyana

🕒 Daily 7–6 (5 in winter)

🍴 Café (£) opposite temple entrance

🚌 Luxor travel agency excursions and taxi are the preferred ways to get to Abydos

🚉 Train connections from Cairo and Luxor

✋ Cheap

↔ Dandara (➤ 74) if travelling from Luxor, Sohag (➤ 75)

❓ Check security arrangements before travelling

The reliefs found in Seti I's temple at Abydos are some of the most beautiful and exquisite in Egypt

Abydos, dedicated to the god Osiris, was a place of pilgrimage for almost two thousand years. Today it is one of the most remarkable archaeological sites.

Abydos is one of the oldest Egyptian settlements, founded long before the Dynastic period (3050 BC), and for thousands of years it was a place of pilgrimage. According to legend, Osiris, god of the underworld, was buried here, and a gap in the nearby hills was the gateway to the underworld. A burial in Abydos, therefore, was considered a good way of ensuring an after-life. Early Egyptian kings built symbolic graves in the desert and those who could were either buried there, had commemorative stones raised in their honour or had their mummies brought on pilgrimage after their death.

Most of ancient Abydos has disappeared or is yet to be excavated. The main attraction is the Temple of Seti I, a magnificent white-marble building of the 14th century BC. There are many inscriptions and images, while reliefs on the walls of the Second Hypostyle Hall are among the finest of the New Kingdom, with a subtlety and vividness that was later lost. The temple's outer hall and façade were finished by Seti's son, Ramses II, who also built a smaller temple some 300m away (not always accessible). Before visiting that, however, go out of the back of the temple to the Osirion or Cenotaph, a strange subterranean building, now often submerged by rising ground-water. A sarcophagus was found here (although Seti was buried in the Valley of the Kings, ➤ 18), which was perhaps part of a ritual unification of the pharaoh and the god of the dead.

2
El-Ahram & Abu'l Hol (Pyramids & Sphinx)

The pyramids at Giza are the most instantly recognisable monuments in the world, while the nearby Sphinx retains its aura of mystique.

The sound and light show gives an insight into the story of King Khufu

There are more than 80 pyramids along the plateau above the Nile valley between Giza and Faiyum, but the three large pyramids at Giza are the most famous and most impressive, built at the apogee of Old Kingdom power. There had been other pyramids before and it is interesting to trace their development from the beginning with Djoser's Step Pyramid at Saqqara (➤ 48), through Snefru's Bent and Red Pyramids at Dahshur (➤ 46) to the geometrically perfect Great Pyramid of Khufu (Cheops) at Giza. Khufu's was the first of the three main pyramids to be built and is the largest, originally 146.6m high (it has now shrunk to 137.5m) and built out of 2,300,000 blocks weighing an average of 2.5 tonnes each. His son Khafre (Chephren) built the Second Pyramid (136.4m high) and gave the Sphinx his face, while Chephren's son Menkaure (Mycerinus) built the third, only 62m high. Around each pyramid there are the remains of the smaller pyramids of the royal families.

The question of who built the Sphinx and why is still unresolved. The massive statue, cut out of the hillside, with a lion's body and a man's head, has attracted more speculation than almost any other monument in Egypt. The only thing that is certain is that it was the first colossal statue of a pharaoh and it is believed that the face on it is that of the Pharaoh Chephren, to whose pyramid it was connected by a covered walkway.

✚ G28C4

✉ Giza plateau, 16km southwest of Cairo

🌐 Site daily 7AM-7:30PM (interior of Great Pyramid 8:30-4:30)

🍽 Café (£) near Sphinx, restaurant (££–£££) at Mena House Hotel

🚌 900 and 80, minibus 82

ℹ Opposite Mena House Hotel ☎ 02-385 0259

✋ Expensive to enter the site and the Pyramid of Khafre, extra ticket expensive to enter the Pyramid of Khufu and moderate to enter the Pyramid of Menkaure

↔ Solar Boat Museum (➤ 47)

❓ Son et lumière show in several languages at the Sphinx daily ☎ 02-385 2880 for information

17

3
Biban el-Muluk
(Valley of the Kings)

The secluded valley of the New Kingdom was known as the 'place of truth'

For 500 years some of Egypt's most famous pharaohs were buried in splendour in fascinating tombs in the Valley of the Kings.

One of the high points of ancient Egyptian history occurred when the princes of Thebes (Luxor) established what is known as the New Kingdom (1570–1070 BC). Previous pharaohs had been buried in pyramids, which had proved easy to rob. Theban pharaohs, who believed their future life depended on keeping their mummies and grave goods intact, had themselves buried in the hills. The tombs were literally cut out of the rock and some are masterpieces of engineering: Seti I's tomb is 100m long, while KV5, the tomb of the sons of Ramses II, currently under excavation, has so far revealed more than a hundred chambers. The walls were covered with inscriptions and decorations, many of which were there to instruct the pharaoh on how to reach the underworld. Tombs were filled with gold and precious objects, protected by deep pits and hidden beneath the valley's rubble. All were broken into in antiquity.

Seti I's tomb is considered to be the finest in the valley, by those who have been lucky enough to see it – it has been closed for some years (Horemheb's No 57, is similar in design if not decor). Tombs are regularly closed and numbers are often restricted, as in Tutankhamun's, to minimise damage. The boy-king's tomb is of interest because of the romance surrounding its discovery and because the mummy is still there. After the tomb was opened by Howard Carter in 1922, several people who visited the site or were involved in its discovery died mysteriously, said to be caused by the curse of the pharaoh. Amongst the more heavily decorated tombs are those of Ramses IV (No 2), Ramses VI (No 9), and Ramses III (No 11), while that of Tuthmosis III (No 34), high up the valley, is the most challenging to reach.

✚ 29D2

✉ West Bank, beyond el-Gurna

🕐 Daily 7–5 (6–7 in summer)

🍴 Café (£) at the valley entrance

🚌 Taxis only, or rented bicycles

ℹ Corniche el-Nil, Luxor
☎ 095-373924

✋ Moderate; expensive for Tutankhamun

↔ Deir el-Bahri (➤ 70), Ramesseum (➤ 73)

❓ Ticket office at the crossroads after the Colossi of Memnon, where you will be told which tombs are closed for restoration

4

Deir Sant Katarin (St Catherine's Monastery)

The monastery is holy to Jews, Christians and Muslims, and is built on the site where it is believed God gave Moses the Ten Commandments.

✝ 29D4

✉ Sinai desert, 450km from Cairo, 140km from Dahab

☎ Head office: St Catherine Protectorate 062-470 032, fax 062-470 033

🕐 Mon–Thu, Sat 9-12. Closed Fri, Sun and public holidays

🍴 Café/restaurant (£)

🚌 Buses from Cairo, Sharm el-Sheikh, Dahab and Nuweiba to the village, 2km from the monastery. Taxi to monastery or pleasant walk

✈ Air Sinai flights to St Catherine from Cairo

♿ Few

✋ Free

❓ Good guidebook and local walking guides available at the monastery. Special permission needed to visit the Chapel of the Burning Bush.

According to the scriptures, when Moses went up towards Mount Sinai to receive the Ten Commandments, God spoke to him through a burning bush. The monastery was founded on the supposed site of the bush in AD 527, on the orders of Byzantine Emperor Justinian. Unlike other monasteries in Egypt, St Catherine belongs to the Greek Orthodox Church and is rich in traditions, one being to hide most daily rituals from visitors. The monastery's icon collection is one of the most important in the world, covering 1,400 years of painting, including the period when Byzantine Christians were banned from producing images of the Holy Family or saints (AD 746–842) – an injunction that isolated Sinai ignored.

Icons are shown in the narthex of the main church, an original, Justinian granite building that incorporates the Chapel of the Burning Bush. Inside the church, through wonderful 6th-century cedarwood doors, icons of the saints are hung on and around twelve magnificent pillars and candles are lit under their images on their name day. The iconostasis (altar screen) is a later 17th-century work, but beyond it in the sanctuary there is one of the masterpieces of Byzantine art, a 6th-century mosaic of the Transfiguration. Outside the church a bush grows which, in spite of local legend, is not the one mentioned in the Bible.

The exceptional 6th-century mosaic of the Transfiguration of Christ was executed like a painting

19

5
Karnak

🕂 29D3

✉ 2.5km north of Luxor centre

🕐 Daily 6–5:30 (open till 6:30 in summer)

🍴 Café (£) by the Sacred Lake

🚌 Minibuses from Luxor centre

ℹ Corniche el-Nil, Luxor ☎ 095-373294

✋ Moderate

↔ Luxor Temple (➤ 67), Luxor Museum (➤ 68), Mummification Museum (➤ 68)

❓ *Son et lumière* show (a walking tour of the temple) 3 or 4 times daily (recommended)

Opposite: *the towering columns of the hypostyle hall*
Below: *the Processional Way, lined with ram-headed sphinxes*

No other religious centre matches Karnak for scale and grandeur. Here, for 1,500 years, the priests offered prayers to the god Amun.

Amun was the local god of Thebes long before the New Kingdom, but his status grew along with that of the Theban princes. By the end of the New Kingdom the priests of Amun owned huge estates and controlled shipping, farming and industry. Their empire within an empire was controlled from the precinct of Amun in Karnak and at its centre stood the temple, embellished over the centuries as pharaohs wished to show goodwill towards the god. The result is one of the world's most extraordinary religious sites.

Karnak is a complex with several temple compounds, which can be confusing and overwhelming to visit. After entering through the 43m-high outer pylon, walk to the core of the complex, the Temple of Amun. Dedicated to the triad of Thebes, the gods Amun, Mut and Khonsu, it has a wonderful 'forest' of pillars, built by Ramses II. Continuing straight through the halls you will come to the sanctuary where the image of Amun lived and where, as the images on the walls show, daily offerings were made. Retracing your steps, turn left out of the inner sanctuary to the Cachette Court, where a massive cache of statues was found, and continue to the Sacred Lake. From here, on the *son et lumière* stand, you can see over the compound. If you have time, stroll through the Open Air Museum, the Northern Enclosure with the Temple of Mut, and the Southern Enclosure.

6
Khan el-Khalili, Cairo

✝ 33D4

✉ Off Sharia el-Azhar and Sharia el-Muski

🕐 Morning to evening (many shops closed Fri prayers and Sun)

🍴 Several cafés and restaurants (£–££)

🚌 Buses from Tahrir

ℹ️ 5 Sharia Adly, Downtown ☎ 02-391 3454

↔ El-Azhar (➤ 34), Bayt el-Suhaymi (➤ 36), Mosques of Qalawun, el-Nasir and Barquq (➤ 41), Sayyidna el-Husayn (➤ 42), Wikala el-Ghouri (➤ 43)

❓ The cafés around Midan el-Husayn are popular in the evening for a mint tea or a waterpipe; the bazaar is especially crowded during *moulids* (➤ 116)

Café terraces are the perfect place to watch the world go by

The warren of alleys brings a touch of the Arabian nights to Cairo, in which shopping is just part of the sensory adventure.

The original *khan* (merchants' inn and storehouse) was built in 1382 and quickly become the focus of the city's international trade. Although it was reconstructed in the 16th century something of the spirit of the original place is still there, as people from all over the world meet to talk and trade.

Officially Khan el-Khalili now refers to a single street, but generally it is used for the shopping area between the Mosque of Sayyidna el-Husayn (➤ 43) and Muzz lidin Allah, one of the Islamic city's main streets. The main alley connecting them, el-Bedestane, is typical with its mix of cheap souvenirs and treasures, where imported Chinese junk sits alongside expensive jewellery and Lalique glass. In a smaller alley to the left of el-Bedestane, coming from el-Husayn, Fishawi's café claims not to have closed since 1773 – not quite true, as you might find, but it is one of the area's social centres.

In the alleys of the Khan el-Khalili there are silversmiths, copper beaters, leather workers and carpet sellers. At the bottom of el-Bedestane, turn right onto the street of Muzz lidin Allah, which leads to the old *souk* el-Nahassin (the copper and gold market) where you can buy wonderful copper trays and gold jewellery. Heading the other way along this extraordinary street, past the old baths, an alley running alongside the Mosque of Barsbay leads past kohl and perfume sellers to the spice market.

7

Mathaf el-Masri
(Egyptian Museum), Cairo

The Egyptian Museum is one of the world's great storehouses of antiquities, and a visit is essential for understanding the glory of the ancient Egyptians.

🕂 32B4

✉ Midan Tahrir, Cairo

☎ 02-575 4319

🕐 Sat–Thu 9-4:45, Fri 9–11:15, 1:30–4

🍴 Several restaurants and cafés outside the museum (£–£££)

Ⓜ Sadat

🚌 Many buses from Midan Tahrir

♿ Few

🖐 Moderate; video permission very expensive; royal mummies expensive–very expensive

↔ Gezira (➤ 37)

Left: *beautiful jewellery from the treasure of Tutankhamun*

Below: *the amazing golden death mask of the boy-king Tutankhamun*

Only part of the museum's collection is on display, but what there is to see is more than anyone could take in on a single visit, so save time to return. The ground-floor galleries are laid out in rough chronological order (though unfortunately not numerically, No 1 is not the oldest), allowing you to walk clockwise from the entrance and have an overview of three thousand years of Egyptian art. Immediately in front of the entrance there is a changing exhibition of masterpieces and in the central atrium gallery there are monumental pieces, including pyramid tops and a magnificent Amarna floor.

The upper floor is devoted to treasures, most of them found in tombs. The staircase in gallery 1 leads directly into the most popular collection, the unique treasures of Tutankhamun. Here, filling several galleries, are the 1,700 grave goods found in his tomb, from the solid gold mask to thrones, headrests, exquisite boxes and a series of golden chariots. The amount of Tutankhamun treasures on display can overwhelm, but save some energy for other galleries, which are arranged according to subjects, from models (boats, houses, farming scenes, warriors) to the lifelike Graeco-Roman portraits (room 14). Part of the pleasure here is finding the unexpected, like a 3,000-year-old toilet seat or a full-size wooden statue. The mummies of several important pharaohs, including Ramses II, are on show in room 52 (separate ticket required).

8
el-Nil (the Nile)

Cruises on the Nile
A variety of boats sail on the Nile, from simple *feluccas* to five-star cruise-boats, but most offer the same itinerary. Sailing between Luxor and Aswan, they take in the sights in both towns and stop at the temples of Esna, Edfu and Kom Ombo on the way. Most cruises take three or four days, although some take five and visit the temple of Dandera. You can also travel down to Cairo, which takes 10 days. Delays may occur at the narrow Esna lock, where boats often have to join a long queue waiting to pass through, so some companies transfer passengers to a sister boat waiting on the other side.

This great river may no longer be Egypt's communication nerve, but it is still the country's lifeline and one of the things that draws people here.

The Nile is the world's longest river and one of the most beautiful. For the last half of its course it receives neither tributaries nor regular rainfall yet in midsummer every year it used to rise in Egypt until it burst its banks and flooded the valley. Villages were built on mounds and ancient writers described them as looking like islands. When the river finally subsided it left a thick deposit of mud on the land, producing fertile ground on which seeds were immediately planted. Some years the river rose so high it destroyed villages and towns, while in others it didn't rise high enough to produce a good crop and people went hungry. Ancient Egyptians worshipped the Nile as a god and hoped for its benevolence.

The source wasn't discovered until the 1850s, when the British explorers Burton and Speke reached Lake Victoria. As a result of knowledge gained about the river, two dams were built (1902 and 1971) to control the flow of water to the valley. The dams and the resultant Lake Nasser, the world's largest reservoir, have ended the flooding and made several crops a year possible, although the farmland is now suffering from a lack of fertilising silt. With the Nile tamed, river travel now almost exclusively for tourists and more people moving from the country to the city, it is tempting to think that the river no longer has significance, but the Nile is as much a part of Egyptian life now as it was in ancient times.

Herodotus' claim that Egypt is a gift from the Nile is still valid today

24

9

Philae Temples, Aswan

*Philae reveals the glory of ancient Egypt's late
flourish under the Greeks and Romans. It is also
one of Egypt's most romantic sites.*

🕀	29D2
✉	Agilkia Island, 9km south of Aswan
🕐	Daily 8–4 (7–5 in summer)
🍴	Café (£) on the shore
🚖	Taxi from Aswan
🚢	Regular boats from the riverbank
🛈	Corniche el-Nil, Aswan ☎ 097-323 297
✋	Moderate–expensive
↔	Aswan Dam (➤ 79)
❓	Daily *son et lumière* show (recommended). Details at the site or tourist office

*Trajan's Kiosk with its
marvellous carved
columns was designed as
the formal entrance to the
Temple of Isis*

The temples, shrines and kiosks of Philae Island were
moved to the nearby Agilkia Island between 1972 and
1980 to protect them from the rising Nile water caused by
the Aswan dams. As part of the massive operation Agilkia
was shaped to make a convincing replica of Philae Island.
The main temple at Philae was dedicated to Osiris's wife
Isis, who was worshipped throughout the Mediterranean
world in Roman times and whose cult survived here until
AD 551, when it was replaced by that of the Virgin Mary.

Arriving at the island by boat is a wonderful experience.
From the landing, long colonnades lead up to the pylon of
the Temple of Isis, which was built during the late
Ptolemaic and early Roman era. The left-hand opening
leads into a 3rd century BC Birth House, dedicated to
Horus, child of Isis and Osiris. The main opening leads to a
second pylon and the temple, which lost much of its
decoration when it was converted into a church around
AD 553. The upper floor has interesting reliefs of Osiris,
who was worshipped in mysterious rites here. The nearby
Temple of Hathor, the deity associated with music, has a
unique image of gods playing instruments. From the Kiosk
of Trajan, originally built as a gateway to the island, there
are beautiful views across the lake to the site of the
original island, now submerged.

10
Sultan Hasan Mosque-Madrasa, Cairo

  33C3

Sharia el-Qal'a

Daily 8–5 (open till 6 in summer)

Open-air café (£) next door

54 from Midan el-Tahrir

Moderate

Bayt el-Kritliya (➤ 36), Citadel (➤ 41), Ibn Tulun Mosque (➤ 37)

The simple beauty and grand scale of this 14th-century mosque makes it one of the most admired of Islamic monuments.

Sultan Hasan was the seventh of Sultan an-Nasir Muhammad's eight sons and was 12 years old when he became sultan of Egypt in 1347. Four years later he was imprisoned in the *harem* by a younger brother. After three years of *harem* life, he was restored to the throne, where he stayed for nearly seven years before being murdered. In his life he knew wealth and debauchery, but Sultan Hasan will always be remembered for his teaching mosque (*madrasa*), one of the largest and finest in the world.

The mosque was the centre of the community, accommodating students of four separate schools of Islamic law. The original design had four minarets but only three were built. One fell in 1361, killing many people; another fell in 1659 and was replaced by a smaller minaret. The sole survivor is 81.6m high, one of the tallest in the city. The sultan intended to be buried here, but the tomb is empty, as his body disappeared. The tomb chamber is decorated with marble and wood, with a blue and gold wooden frieze around the room. The masterpiece, however, is the main prayer space, a massive, perfectly proportioned courtyard with four huge arches leading off it in symmetry, creating four open-sided rooms. Between them are doors to the law schools and in the centre there is a domed fountain for ablutions. Beautiful glass lamps (some now in the Islamic Art Museum, ➤ 38) were used to illuminate the prayer recesses.

The best time to view Sultan Hasan's mosque-madrasa is in the morning, when the sun lights up the mausoleum and the courtyard

What to See

Above: the alabaster sphinx staring
over the ruins of Memphis
Right: a visit to the Coptic Museum
is a must

EGYPT

Mediterranean

Salûm
Sidi Barrani
Mersa Matrûh
Rashid (Rosetta)
el Iskandarîya (Alexandria)
el
Damanhûr
Sîdi Abd el Rahman
War Cemetery
Abusir
Baramous
el Álamein
Bir Hooker
Libyan Plateau
Wadi el-Natrûn
Pyramids & Sph
Mem
Saq
Birket Qarûn
Faiyûm Oasis
el Faiyûn
Beni

Qattâra Depression

Siwa Oasis
Siwa

Maghâgh
Beni Mazâr

Baharîya Oasis
Bawiti

el Minya

White Desert

Tuna el Gebel
Malla
Dairi
Deir el Muharraq
Man

Qasr Farafra
Farafra Oasis

Western Desert

Libyan Desert

Dakhla Oasis
el Qasr
Mût
el Khârga

el K
O
Bârîs

465m
▲
Abu Ballas

Gilf Kebir Plateau

| A | B | C |

| (HJK) Jordan | (L-R) Libya | (SD) Sudan |
| (IL) Israel | (SA) Saudi Arabia | (SYR) Syria |

(L-R)

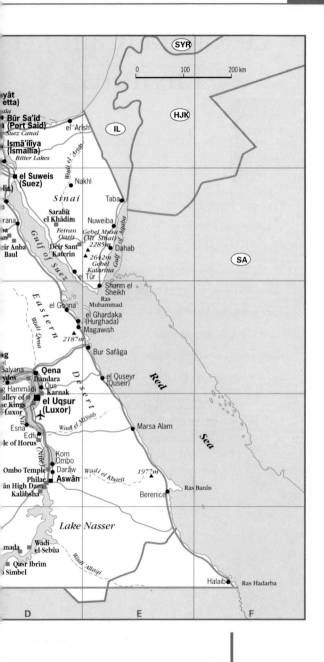

El-Kahira (Cairo) & Environs

The origins of Cairo can be traced back through the 4th century BC capital of Memphis to the Roman fortress at Babylon. The Arab city of Cairo was founded in AD 969 as a palace-enclave, but grew into a great medieval city, enriched by trade with Venice and the East. It is primarily an Islamic city, centred around the Mosque of el-Azhar and the shrine of the city's patron saint, Sayyidna el-Husayn. The explosion of trade in the 19th century between Europe and its Asian empires led to the building of the Suez Canal and also saw the construction of much of what is now Downtown Cairo. The city has grown rapidly in recent years and now spreads far into the desert.

> *'Travellers tell us that there is not on earth's face aught fairer than Cairo and her Nile...' Quoth my father, 'Whoso hath not seen Cairo hath not seen the world.'*

Tale of the Jewish Doctor, from the
Thousand and One Nights

Cairo

Cairo can be a challenging place to visit for the first time. More than 15 million people, several thousand years of history and a mixture of cultural influences from Africa, Asia and Europe add up to a serious assault on the senses. But Cairo somehow reconciles its extremes; great beauty with urban and industrial sprawl, affluence with poverty, the long shadow of the past with the promise of the future. Although it makes demands on its visitors (the traffic, pollution and hassles), its citizens make up for that by being some of the most hospitable and humorous people in the world.

The Nile functions as Cairo's lung, and on hot summer nights families flock to the river for a breath of fresh air

What to See in Cairo

AMR IBN EL-AS MOSQUE ✪✪

Amr, the Arab general who conquered Christian Egypt in AD 641, established the city of Fustat here, near the Roman fortress of Babylon. By the 12th century this was one of the world's wealthiest cities, but it was burned to avoid it falling to the Crusaders – the fire lasted for 54 days – and has remained a mound of rubble ever since. Amr's Mosque, the first in Egypt, was later restored and underwent many subsequent renovations, the last being in the 1970s. The pleasure now is to spot the old features, particularly columns reused from churches and temples. In the far left corner lies Amr's son, Abdallah. Originally buried inside his house, his tomb was incorporated into the mosque during a 9th-century redevelopment.

- 🞤 32B1
- ✉ 500m north of Mari Girgis, Coptic Cairo
- ⏰ Daily 9–4 (closed 12–1 Fri)
- Ⓜ Mari Girgis
- 💲 Cheap
- ↔ el-Muallaqa church (➤ 40), Ben Ezra Synagogue (➤ 36), Coptic Museum (➤ 40)

31

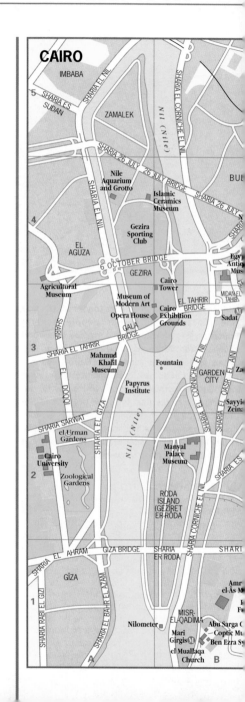

CAIRO

IMBABA

ZAMALEK

EL AGUZA

Nile Aquarium and Grotto

Islamic Ceramics Museum

Gezira Sporting Club

Agricultural Museum

GEZIRA

Cairo Tower

Museum of Modern Art

Opera House

Cairo Exhibition Grounds

Mahmud Khalil Museum

Papyrus Institute

el-Urman Gardens

Cairo University

Zoological Gardens

Manyal Palace Museum

RODA ISLAND (GEZIRET ER-RODA)

GIZA BRIDGE

GIZA

Nilometer

MISR-EL-QADIMA

Mari Girgis

el Muallaqa Church

Amr el-Âs M

Abu Sarga C

Coptic Mu

Ben Ezra Sy

SHARIA EL NIL

SHARIA ES SUDAN

SHARIA EL CORNICHE EL NIL

NIL (Nile)

SHARIA 26 JULY

26 JULY BRIDGE

SHARIA EL NIL

6 OCTOBER BRIDGE

EL TAHRIR BRIDGE

GALA BRIDGE

SHARIA EL TAHRIR

EL DOQQI

SHARIA

SHARIA EL GIZA

SHARIA SARWAT

SHARIA EL TAHRIR

NIL (Nile)

SHARIA EL CORNICHE EL NIL

SHARIA EL QASR EL AINI

GARDEN CITY

Sayyid Zeina

Fountain

SHARIA EL AHRAM

SHARIA RABI EL GIZI

SHARIA EL BAHR EL AZAM

SHARIA ER RODA

SHARIA CORNICHE EL NIL

SHARI

Egy Antiq Mus

MIDAN EL TAHRIR

Sadat

BUL

Fountain

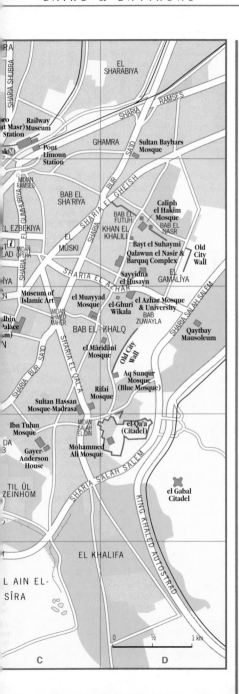

EL
SHARABIYA

SHARIA RAMSES

...RA

SHARIA SHUBRA

Railway
Museum
Station

...ro
(...t Masr)

...uk

Pont
Limoun
Station

GHAMRA

SAID

Sultan Baybars
Mosque

MIDAN
RAMSES

...GUMHURIYA

BAB EL
SHA'RIYA

SHARIA EL GHEISH

BUR

Caliph
el Hakim
Mosque

EL EZBEKIYA

SHARIA

EL
MÚSKI

BAB EL
FUTUH

KHAN EL
KHALILI

BAB EL
NASR

Old
City
Wall

i
MIDAN
OPERA

...LAD

Bayt el Suhaymi

Qalawun el Nasir &
Barquq Complex

...ÍYA

SHARIA EL AZHAR

Sayyidna
el Husayn

EL
GAMALÍYA

...N

Museum of
Islamic Art

el Muayyad
Mosque

el-Ghuri
Wikala

el Azhar Mosque
& University

SHARIA SALAH SALEM

...lbn
...Palace
...m)

MIDAN
AHMED
MAHER

BAB EL - KHALQ

BAB
ZUWAYLA

SHARIA BUR SAID

el Mâridâni
Mosque

Old City
Wall

Qaytbay
Mausoleum

SHARIA EL QAL'A

Aq Sunqur
Mosque
(Blue Mosque)

Rifai
Mosque

Sultan Hassan
Mosque-Madrasa

...DA
...3

Ibn Tulun
Mosque

Gayer
Anderson
House

MIDAN
SALAH
EL DIN

el-Qa'a
(Citadel)

Mohammed
Ali Mosque

TIL ÛL
ZEINHOM

SHARIA SALAH SALEM

el Gabal
Citadel

KING KHALED AUTOSTRAD

...M

EL KHALIFA

L AIN EL-
SÎRA

0   ½   1 km

C   D

Above: *for more than 1,000 years el-Azhar has offered free education and board to students from all over the Islamic world*

EL-AZHAR MOSQUE AND UNIVERSITY   ✪✪

El-Azhar ('the most blooming'), founded in AD 971, was the first mosque in the Fatimid city, and claims to be the oldest university in the world. As Egypt's supreme theological authority, the Sheikh of el-Azhar plays a significant role in national politics. The mosque is entered through the remarkable 18th-century Barber's Gate, where students traditionally had their heads shaved. Beyond is a large *sahn* or courtyard, part of the original 10th-century design, overlooked by three minarets. To the right is a Mameluke *madrasa* (Kuranic school), with apartments for Kuranic students. The oldest part of the building is the east *liwan* (hall), in which many ancient alabaster pillars were reused. The university now occupies several large modern blocks behind the mosque.

BAB ZUWAYLA AND OTHER CITY GATES   ✪✪

Bab Zuwayla, built in 1092 and also known as Bab el-Mitwalli, was the southern gate of the Fatimid city. From the terrace between its imposing twin towers, Mameluke sultans watched the departure of the annual caravan of pilgrims to Mecca. After the Turkish conquest, the last Mameluke sultan was hung from this gate, and in the 19th century a saint, Mitwalli el-Qutb, was known to perform miracles here. Adjacent to the gates is the 15th-century el-Muayyad Mosque with a peaceful, tree-shaded courtyard. On the northern side of the Fatimid city are the Bab el-Futuh (Gate of Conquests) and Bab el-Nasr (Gate of Victory), joined by a 200m-long tunnel with fine brick work.

> ### DID YOU KNOW?
>
> Adjacent to the Bab el-Futuh is the early 11th-century mosque of Caliph el-Hakim. El-Hakim was a strange character. As he loved night-time, he decreed that this would be the time for work while the days were for sleeping. He hated women so much they were not allowed to go out and cobblers for women were closed down. He also had all Cairo's dogs killed because they made too much noise. After his death, the Druze proclaimed that he would return as the Messiah.

Walk between Two City Gates

Start at Bab Zuwayla (➤ 34) and walk along Sharia el-Muzz lidin Allah.

Tip the guardian at el-Muayyad Mosque (➤ 34) on the left, to climb up the minaret for views over the old city.

Back on the street, turn left and continue past a little square where cotton is sold, to the 19th-century Sabil-Kuttab of Tusun Pasha. A hundred metres on stands the ruined 12th-century Fakahani Mosque. Fifty metres further, on the left, are the city's last two tarboush (fez) shops.

Just before the intersection with Sharia el-Azhar is the Ghuriya complex, with the 16th-century Mosque-Madrasa of el-Ghuri (left) and the Mausoleum of el-Ghuri and the el-Ghuri Palace (right), now used for performances of the Whirling Dervishes (➤ 113).

Cross via the walking bridge and continue along the more touristy end of Sharia el-Muzz.

After 50m, around the Madrasa of Barsbey, shops sell spices, perfume, fetishes and folk cures. After the intersection with el-Muski, the street turns into the Gold Bazaar and further on into the Coppersmiths' Bazaar. Past this to the right is the Madrasa of Sultan Ayyub and to the left the superb Qalawun, el-Nasir and Barquq complex (➤ 41).

With Qasr Bashtak on the right, take the left-hand fork at the lovely drinking fountain Sabil-Kuttab of Kathkuda. One block past the 12th-century Mosque of el-Aqmar, 70m further to the right, turn right into Darb el-Asfar for Bayt el-Suhaymi (➤ 36). Return to the main street and turn right, past the el-Silahdar Mosque. Continue through the lemon and garlic market to the Mosque of el-Hakim, built against the Northern Walls and the Bab el-Futuh (➤ 34).

Distance
1½km

Time
2 hours without stops, at least half day with stops

Start point
Bab Zuwayla
✚ 33D3

End point
Bab el-Futuh
✚ 33D4

The tree-shades courtyard of the el-Muayyad Mosque offers a peaceful retreat from the bustle of the souks

35

🕇 33C2
✉ 4 Midan Ahmed Ibn Tulun, Sayyda Zaynab
☎ 02-364 7822
🕐 Daily 8–4. Closed 12–1 Fri
🚌 174; minibus No 54 from Midan Tahrir
📝 Moderate (combined ticket with Islamic Art Museum, ➤ 38)
↔ Ibn Tulun Mosque (➤ 37), Citadel (➤ 41), Sultan Hasan Mosque-Madrasa (➤ 26)

🕇 33D4
✉ 19 Darb el-Asfar, el-Gamaliya
🕐 Daily 9–4
🚌 66
📝 Cheap
↔ Bab el-Futuh (➤ 34), Qalawun complex (➤ 41), Khan el-Khalili (➤ 22)

The synagogue was also used for keeping valuable sacred documents which included one of the oldest known Torahs in the world

---

🕇 32B1
✉ Mari Girgis, Coptic Cairo
🕐 Daily 9–5
🚇 Mari Girgis
♿ Few
📝 Free, donations welcome
↔ El-Muallaqa (➤ 40), Coptic Museum (➤ 40)

BAYT EL-KRITILIYA (GAYER-ANDERSON HOUSE) ✪✪

The Gayer-Anderson House, two adjoining 16th- and 17th-century mansions, is an orientalist's dream. The orientalist in question was a British major, R J Gayer-Anderson, who lived here from 1935 to 1942 and collected ancient Egyptian and Oriental art. The spacious and harmoniously decorated *qa'a* (men's reception room) appeared in the 1977 James Bond film *The Spy Who Loved Me*, and is one of the finest such rooms in Cairo. The *harem* (women's and children's quarters) includes a succession of finely decorated rooms, a roof terrace to take the air and secret windows which allowed the women to look onto the *qa'a* without being seen.

BAYT EL-SUHAYMI ✪✪

This remarkable 16th- and 17th-century house, which belonged to a wealthy merchant and his many wives and concubines, is a labyrinth of rooms for the men followed by rooms for the *harem* (women and children). They are all beautifully decorated and perfectly air-conditioned in traditional style, centred around a cool, peaceful courtyard where it is pleasant to linger for a while.

BEN EZRA SYNAGOGUE ✪✪

The splendidly restored Ben Ezra Synagogue is the oldest surviving synagogue in Egypt. Formerly the 4th-century Church of St Michael, it is built in basilica style with three naves and a hidden altar, and the intricate decoration is not unlike that of the nearby churches. Copts believe that this was where Moses was found in a basket, while Jews claim that Jeremiah preached here in the 6th century. Services are no longer held.

GEZIRA ✪✪

Gezira, the largest island on the Nile in Cairo, is divided in two by the 6th of October Bridge. The exclusive residential area Zamalek, on the northern side, has many up-market shops and restaurants and is home to the Gezira Sporting Club (➤ 115), founded in 1877 by the British Army. The landmarks on the Gezira (southern) end are the Cairo Tower and the Opera House. The 187m-high Cairo Tower, built in the late 1950s, has a revolving restaurant and, on a clear day, sweeping views over Cairo to the desert. The Opera House (➤ 113), a gift from Japan, was built in 1988 to replace the one that burned down in 1971. In its grounds is the Museum of Egyptian Modern Art and across the road is the Mokhtar Museum, which shows the work of Egypt's most famous 20th-century sculptor.

🕂 32A4
✉ Gezira Island
🕑 Cairo Tower daily 9AM–midnight; Modern Art and Mokhtar Museum Tue–Sun 10–1, 5–9; Fri 10–12, 5–9. Closed Mon
🍴 Café/restaurant on top of Cairo Tower (££)
🚇 Mari Girgis
🚌 Minibus 54
♿ Few
💰 Cairo Tower moderate, museums cheap

IBN TULUN MOSQUE ✪✪✪

Built by Ahmed Ibn Tulun in AD 876–9, this exquisite mosque is a rare example of the classical period in Islamic architecture (9th to 10th centuries). The peaceful courtyard, with its simple grandeur, was built as a vast, open-air prayer hall – this was the city's central mosque and is now its oldest functioning Islamic monument. The 2km-long sycamore-wood frieze is said to contain one-fifth of the Koran in Kufic inscriptions. The unusual minaret with an outside spiral staircase was inspired by the architecture of Samarra in Iraq, where Tulun grew up, although local lore has it that the sultan absent-mindedly rolled up a piece of paper and handed it to the architect as being the design.

🕂 33C2
✉ Midan Ahmed Ibn Tulun
🕑 Daily 8–6
♿ Few
💰 Cheap
🔁 Gayer-Anderson House (➤ 36), Citadel (➤ 41), Sultan Hasan Mosque-Madrasa (➤ 26)

Above: *if there is only time to visit one mosque in Cairo, it should be Ibn Tulun's, which stands out for its bold simplicity*

KHAN EL-KHALILI (➤ 22, TOP TEN)

33C3

Sharia Bur Said on intersection with Sharia el Qal'a

02-390 9930

Sat–Thu 9–4, Fri 9–11, 2–4

Café in garden (£)

Few

Moderate

Bab Zuwayla (➤ 34), Tentmakers' Bazaar (➤ 107)

Ticket is also valid for Gayer-Anderson House (➤ 36)

32A4

Gezira Art Centre, 1 Sharia el-Marsafy, Zamalek

02-340 8211

10–1, 5–7

Few

Free

Complex includes several art galleries, an open-air theatre and a cinema

Intricate geometrical screens decorate the sumptuous interior of the early 20th-century Manyal Palace

MATHAF EL-ISLAMI (MUSEUM OF ISLAMIC ART) ✪✪

This rare and extensive collection of Islamic arts looks rather dusty, but holds the key to understanding the architecture of Islamic Cairo. Seeing the appalling state of many Cairene mosques and palaces, Khedive Tewfiq founded a museum of Islamic art in 1880 to salvage parts of derelict buildings. All exhibits are arranged chronologically or by medium, and are dated AH – After the Hegira, when Muhammad is thought to have fled from Mecca to Medina, which is the beginning of the Islamic Calendar (AD 622). Sunni Muslims consider the representation of human and animal figures as idolatry, so there are no statues in the museum and most of the designs are based on floral motifs, geometric patterns and Arab calligraphy. The exception to this rule was the art of the Shi'a Fatimids who allowed birds, animals and scenes from daily life in the decoration of their objects. Amongst the masterpieces are the amazing door from Sayyida Zeynab's mosque (Room 13), a 14th-century Mameluke fountain (Room 5) and fine glass lamps (Room 21).

MATHAF EL-KHAFZ EL- ISLAMI ✪✪
(ISLAMIC CERAMICS MUSEUM)

The domed palace of Prince Amr Ibrahim, a neo-Islamic, 20th-century building, houses a wonderful range of ceramics from all over the Islamic world, put together from the collections of the Egyptian royal family, Prince Amr Ibrahim and the Islamic Art Museum (see above). The well-displayed collection has several rare pieces, including a precious 17th-century porcelain plate from Andalucia and a very fine 16th-century Turkish *mishkaa* or hanging lamp.

MATHAF EL-MASRI (EGYPTIAN MUSEUM)
(➤ 23, TOP TEN)

The Mahmud Khalil Museum is home to an important collection of late 19th- and early 20th-century European paintings

MATHAF MAHMUD KHALIL (MAHMUD KHALIL MUSEUM)

This splendid little museum is home to a superb collection of original French impressionist paintings and fine sculpture, which comes as something of a surprise to tourists, very few of whom visit the place. Little known paintings by the likes of Renoir, Monet, Van Gogh, Pissarro, Gauguin and Ingres, sculptures by artists such as Rodin, as well as Chinese porcelain and jade, were lovingly gathered by Mahmud Khalil, a pre-war agricultural minister, and his French wife. They bequeathed their collection to the state on the condition that it would be displayed in their own Italianate villa, but for many years it was shown in the Prince Amr Ibrahim Palace (➤ 38) and only recently returned to the Khalil house.

32A3
1 Sharia Kafour, Giza, next to the Maglis el-Dawla (State Council)
02-336 2358/76
Tue–Sun 10–5:30. Closed Mon
Very good
Moderate
Gezira (➤ 37)
You need your passport to enter the museum

MATHAF QASR EL-MANYAL (MANYAL PALACE MUSEUM)

Built in an amazing cocktail of architectural styles, from Persian and Moorish to Ottoman and Rococo, this early 20th-century palace belonged to King Farouk's uncle, Prince Muhammad Ali. The Reception Palace is finely decorated with stained glass and colourful tiles, and of the series of rooms upstairs the Syrian Room is the finest, with exquisite inlay of mother-of-pearl. Most rooms in the Royal Residence have wonderful blue tiling, while the Private Museum houses an interesting collection of porcelain, pictures, rugs and copies of the Koran. A bizarre display of dusty and ragged stuffed animals is on show in the Trophies Museum, near the gate. The once magnificent gardens are being restored to their former glory.

32B2
Near el-Gamaa Bridge, Roda Island
Daily 9–4
Few
Cheap

32B1

Coptic Cairo

02-362 8766

Daily 9–4 (closed Fri 11–1)

Café in the garden (£)

Mari Girgis

Moderate

El-Muallaqa (➤ below), Ben Ezra Synagogue (➤ 36)

Opposite: the Mosque of Muhammad Ali in the Citadel

Below: Coptic papyri illustrate how the Copts followed ancient Egyptian techniques and traditions

MATHAF EL-QIBTI (COPTIC MUSEUM)

The Coptic Museum's valuable collection of secular and religious Coptic artefacts, from AD 200–1800, shows fascinating evidence of ancient Egyptian influence on early Christianity. The ground floor of the New Wing is arranged chronologically, starting with early Christian reliefs suggesting that the Christian cross developed from the pharaonic *ankh* (the 'key of life' looped cross). Note also the wonderful frescoes from the 6th-century el-Bawit monastery. Room 6 has the earliest recorded stone pulpit from the 6th-century St Jeremiah monastery in Saqqara, while Room 10 claims to have the oldest surviving book in the world, a 1,600-year-old copy of the Psalms of David. Some magnificent Coptic textiles are on display on the upper floor. The Old Wing, remarkable in itself for the fine woodwork and ceiling carvings, houses some interesting pottery and artefacts from Coptic churches. The towers and walls in the garden were built by Roman Emperor Trajan around AD 130 as part of Babylon.

32B1

Coptic Cairo

Mon–Sat 9–4, Sun 12–4

Mari Girgis

Few

Donations welcome. Well-informed Coptic students often guide visitors round

Coptic Museum (➤ above), Ben Ezra Synagogue (➤ 36)

EL-MUALLAQA (HANGING CHURCH)

The Hanging Church, built over a Roman Gate, is reached via an impressive stairway, which leads to a vestibule where videos of papal sermons and wonderfully kitsch Coptic shrines are on sale. Copts believe that the church was founded in the 4th century, but it could date to at least 300 years after that. The main nave, with a ceiling vaulted like an ark, is separated from the aisles by 16 pillars that probably carried images of saints. The altar areas are hidden by finely carved wooden screens inlaid with ivory and the exquisite marble pulpit is supported by 12 pillars, one for each of the apostles.

EL-QAL'A (CITADEL) ✪✪✪

Realising the difficulty of protecting Cairo, Salah el-Din el-Ayyubi (Saladin) built the Citadel in the 12th century. Its design was strongly influenced by Crusader castles in Palestine and Syria. The most obvious building, seen from many parts of Cairo, is the 19th-century Mosque of Muhammad Ali, inspired by grand Ottoman mosques in Istanbul. Inside, despite the soaring dome, the lack of proportion and the overdone decor are disappointing. The courtyard clock was a gift from King Louis-Philippe of France, in exchange for the Luxor obelisk now in the Place de la Concorde, Paris. Next door is the 14th-century Mosque of el-Nasir with a tiled minaret, and the Gawhara Palace, the former royal quarters, built in a French style. Among several museums, there is the Carriage Museum, the National Police Museum and the Seized Museum.

╋	33D2
⊠	Bab el-Gadid, off Sikkat el Mahgat
⊙	Daily 8–6 summer, 8–5 winter. Closed Fri 11:30–1:30. Museums close 4:30
🍴	Café (£)
🚌	Bus 82 from Midan Tahrir
♿	Few
🖐	Moderate for Muhammad Ali Mosque, moderate extra ticket for museums
↔	Sultan Hasan Mosque-Madrasa (➤ 26), Ibn Tulun Mosque (➤ 37), Bab Zuwayla (➤ 34)

QALAWUN, EL-NASIR AND BARQUQ COMPLEX ✪✪✪

The splendid 185m-long façade of this Mameluke complex is one of Cairo's most wonderful sights. Coming from el-Azhar, the first building is Qalawun's *maristan* (hospital and madhouse) built in 1285 and used as such until 1850. Next door is the beautifully restored and richly decorated mausoleum of Sultan Qalawun and behind it a *madrasa* (Kuranic school). His son el-Nasir Muhammad, who is also buried in this mausoleum, followed his father's plan and built in 1304 a mosque, a *madrasa* and mausoleum next door. Barquq, the first Circassian Mameluke sultan, added his share to it and built in 1386 a fine *khanqah* (religious hostel) and a magnificent *madrasa* behind heavy bronze-plated doors with silver inlay.

╋	33D4
⊠	Bayn el-Qasrayn, Sharia Muzz lidin Allah
⊙	Qalawun mausoleum daily 9–5, el-Nasir daily 9–4, Barquq daily 8–5
🖐	Cheap (plus tips)
↔	Bayt el-Suhaymi (➤ 36), Khan el-Khalili (➤ 22), Sayyidna el-Husayn Mosque (➤ 43), Bab el-Futuh (➤ 34)
❓	The complex is undergoing restoration at the time of writing

41

QASR ABDIN (ABDIN PALACE MUSEUM)

Khedive Ismail built this 500-room palace as part of th
redevelopment of Cairo to accompany the opening of th
Suez Canal in 1869. Four years later he moved the roy
family here from the Citadel, where they lived until th
revolution in 1952 (fulfilling a prophesy that the dynas
would only survive if it stayed in the Citadel). The ma
palace is closed to the public, but in a separate buildin
there are displays of weaponry and suits of armour, as we
as part of the former royal family's impressive collection of
silver, china and crystal. The medal museum contains Kir
Farouk's amusing collection of badges.

- 33C3
- Midan Abdin, Downtown
- 02-391 0042
- Sat–Thu 9–3
- Few
- Moderate
- Wust el-Balad (see opposite), Islamic Art Museum (➤ 38)
- No cameras

QAYTBAY MAUSOLEUM-MADRASA

The grandest building in the Northern Cemetery belonge
to the last powerful Mameluke ruler, Sultan Qaytbay, wh
reigned from 1468 to 1496. This jewel of late Mameluk
architecture is perfect in many ways, with faultless propo
tions, fine carving around the doors and windows and a
elegant minaret. Although the decoration of the madra
(Kuranic school) is amazingly rich, the overall effect is on
of simplicity and harmony, using the primary Islam
designs: calligraphy, arabesque and geometric pattern
The tomb chamber, one of the most impressive in Cairo,
covered by a magnificent huge dome.

- 33D3
- El-Qarafa el-Sharkiya (Northern Cemetery), el-Dirasa
- Daily 9–8
- Minibus No 77 from Tahrir
- Cheap

The perfectly proportioned dome of Qaytbay's mausoleum is decorated with fine polygonal reliefs

The modern mosque of Sayyidna el-Husayn with its Turkish-style minarets was built over an earlier Fatimid mosque

SAYYIDNA EL-HUSAYN MOSQUE ✪

One of Cairo's most sacred mosques dedicated to the Prophet Muhammad's grandson Husayn, who was killed in 680 in Iraq. Although it has been disputed that his head is buried here, Husayn has emerged as the city's patron saint and his mosque attracts Muslims from around the world, particularly during the annual *moulid* (birthday celebration). Cairenes believe the whole area, including the cafés, around the mosque has a special *baraka* (blessing), and so it is a popular place in the evening. Alcohol is forbidden.

🔲 33D4
✉ Midan el-Husayn
🖐 Free
↔ El-Azhar Mosque (➤ 34), Khan el-Khalili (➤ 22), Wikala el-Ghuri (➤ below)
❓ Closed to non-Muslims. *The* place to be or to avoid during major Muslim festivals

SULTAN HASAN MOSQUE-MADRASA (➤ 26, TOP TEN)

WIKALA EL-GHURI ✪✪

This restored Mameluke caravanserai (merchants' inn and storehouse) is an oasis of cool, calm and silence amidst the hubbub of the bazaars and lively streets of the old city. It now provides workshops for craftsmen and studios for painters, some of which can be visited. Traditional crafts are on sale. The 16th-century courtyard is used for theatre and concerts and houses an exhibition of peasant and bedouin crafts.

🔲 33D3
✉ Off Sharia Muzz lidin Allah, near el-Azhar Mosque
🕐 Daily 9–5. Closed Fri
🖐 Cheap
↔ El-Azhar Mosque (➤ 34), Khan el-Khalili (➤ 22)

WUST EL-BALAD (DOWNTOWN) ✪✪

The reconstruction of central Cairo was another of Khedive Ismail's extravagant projects for the inauguration of the Suez Canal in 1869. Impressed with Paris's boulevards, he built elegant avenues like Talaat Harb and Qasr el-Nil. Nowadays the streets are congested and many buildings have been demolished, but a walk downtown still has its rewards, particularly when you look up at the grand 19th-century colonial-style buildings. Midan Tahrir, Cairo's main square, and the Nile Hilton complex were created after the 1952 revolution on the site of the British barracks.

🔲 33B3
🕐 Most shops are closed Sun
🍴 Cafés and restaurants (£–£££)
🚇 Sadat
♿ Few
↔ Egyptian Museum (➤ 23), Gezira (➤ 37)

In the Know

If you only have a short time to visit Egypt and would like to get a real flavour of the country, here are some ideas:

10 Ways to Be a Local

- **Always take time for extensive greetings**: *salaam alaykum, sabah el-ward* (a morning full of roses), *sabah el-yasmin* (a morning of jasmine).
- **Take your time**, and remember to use the expressions *inshallah* (if God wills it), *bukra* (tomorrow) and *ma'alesh* (never mind) as often as you can.
- **Eat** *fuul* (stewed fava beans) for breakfast.
- **Take your shoes off** when visiting mosques.
- **Watch a belly dance** show at 3AM rather than the tourist version at 8PM.
- **Have a joke** or humorous remark for every occasion.
- **Sit on a café terrace** and smoke a *sheesha* (waterpipe).
- **Cheer loudly** at actors when watching a film.
- **Go for a summer evening stroll** on Cairo's Gezira Island.
- **Travel between cities** in communal Peugeot taxis, also known as 'flying coffins'.

Lose yourself watching the water bubble at the bottom of a pipe and then inhale its honey-sweetened smoke

10 Good Places to Have Lunch

- **Andrea (£–££)**, 59-60 Marioutiya Canal, el-Ahram, Giza 02-383 1133. Succulent roast chicken in a peaceful garden (➤ 92).
- **Felfella Garden(£–££)**, 15 Sharia Hoda Shaarawi, Downtown Cairo ☎ 02-392 2833. For *mezze* and stuffed pigeon (➤ 93).
- **Fish Market (££–£££)**, 26 Corniche el-Nil, Alexandria ☎ 03-480 5114. Superb fish and great views (➤ 95).
- **Hassan Bleik (£)**, Opposite 18 Sharia Saad Zaghloul, Alexandria ☎ 03-484 0880. Delicious Lebanese dishes (➤ 95).
- **Marriott Garden (£)**, Marriott Hotel, Zamalek, Cairo ☎ 02- 340 888. Club sandwiches, grills and pizzas in a palace garden (➤ 100).
- **Marsam Hotel (£)**, West Bank, Luxor ☎ 095-372 165. Simple Egyptian food and view of Theban Hills (➤ 97).
- **Naguib Mahfouz Coffee Shop (£)**, 5 el-Badestan alley, Khan el-Khalili, Cairo ☎ 02-590 3788. Watch the crowds in the bazaar (➤ 93).
- **Nora's Floating Restaurant (££)**, Sharia Filastine, Port Said. For a view of the Suez Canal (➤ 98).
- **Sayyadeen (££)**, Mövenpick Hotel, El-Gouna

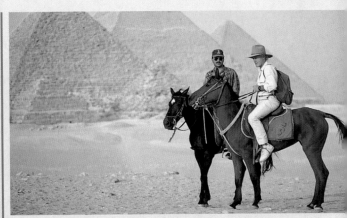

Riding round the pyramids is an exhilarating excursion but the trip is tiring and not recommended for novices

☎ 065-545 160. Excellent fish on the beach (➤ 99).
• **Zephyrion (££)**, 41 Sharia Khaled Ibn Walid, Abu Qir, Alexandria ☎ 03-560 1319. Fish restaurant overlooking the sea (➤ 95).

10
Top Activities

• *Felucca* **sailing** between Aswan and Luxor (➤ 78).
• **Birdwatching** at Wadi Rayan in Faiyum (➤ 46).
• **Desert driving** in the Western Desert (➤ 114).
• **Hot air ballooning** over Luxor with Balloons over Egypt (☎ 095-376516).
• **Swimming** Most luxury hotels allow non-residents to use their pool for a fee.
• **Windsurfing** in the Red Sea, especially Moon Beach Resort, Ras Sudr (☎ & fax 02-336 5103)
• **Hiking** in Sinai (infor-

mation from St Catherine's Protectorate ☎ 062-470 032, fax 062-470 033).
• **Horse riding** at the Pyramids of Giza or on the West Bank in Luxor (stables ➤ 115)
• **Fishing** safaris on Lake Nasser (for information ☎ & fax 097-311 011)

5
Best Markets

• **El-Muski** in Cairo. Busy street market with toys, textiles, stationery, clothes and household goods, Mon–Sat.
• **Souk el-Gimal** in Birqash, 30km northwest of Cairo, on early Monday and Friday mornings. Camels from Sudan are sold, plus goats and saddles.
• **Souk el-Gimal** in Daraw. Sudanese traders sell their camels to local farmers in this colourful market (➤ 80).
• **Tewfiqiya Market**, Downtown, Cairo. Excellent food and

vegetable market.
• **Sharia el-Suq**, Aswan. Laid back market full of fetishes, lovely baskets, silk shawls and stuffed baby crocodiles.

5
Best Views

• Sunset over Islamic and modern Cairo, and the pyramids from the terrace of the Mohammed Ali Mosque (➤ 41).
• Climb the path above Deir el-Bahri (➤ 70) for views over the mortuary temples, fluorescent green sugarcane fields and the Nile in Luxor.
• *Feluccas* catching the wind and Aswan in the background from the Aga Khan Mausoleum (➤ 76)
• Take a room in the Cecil Hotel (➤ 102) with sweeping views over the Corniche in Alexandria.
• See the sun rise over Sinai from the summit of Gebel Musa in St Catherine's Protectorate (➤ 19).

45

What to See Around Cairo

EL-AHRAM AND ABU'L-HOL (PYRAMIDS AND SPHINX) (➤ 17, TOP TEN)

DAHSHUR   ✪✪

Wealthy Cairenes choose the quiet countryside of Dahshur to build their weekend retreats, but it also has two impressive Old Kingdom pyramids, both built by Snefru (*c*2613–1588 BC), the father of Khufu, which give an insight into the evolution of pyramid building. The imposing Bent Pyramid, its shiny white limestone casing more or less intact, is unlike any other pyramid. It rises more steeply than the pyramid of Khufu but suddenly changes to a gentler angle near the top. The Red Pyramid, its sides built at a 43-degree angle, is considered the first 'true' pyramid.

✚ 28C4
✉ 5km south of Saqqara
🕐 Daily 8–5
👖 Moderate
↔ Saqqara (➤ 48–9), Memphis (➤ 47)

EL FAIYUM   ✪✪

Faiyum is surrounded by desert but is not a real oasis as it is connected to the Nile via the Bahr Yusuf. Faiyum town is a dull provincial centre, most famous for its water-wheels, particularly the Seven Waterwheels north of town. Its main attractions lie in its environs, especially Birket Qarun, a salt lake which attracts Cairenes for a rowing session and hunters looking for duck and geese. The waterfalls and freshwater lakes of Wadi Rayan, near the village of Tunis, are an ideal place to swim and watch birds. There are also several ancient sites in the area, including the well-preserved Ptolemaic temple of Qasr Qarum and interesting ruins of a Ptolemaic-Roman town at Kom Aushim (just off the Cairo road).

✚ 28C4
✉ 100km southwest of Cairo
ℹ Sharia Gumhurriya
  ☎ 084-332 296
🍴 Café (£–££) and restaurant (££)
🚌 Frequent buses from Cairo at the Ahmed Helmi terminal behind Ramses Station

Opposite: *Birket Qarun no longer has the crocodiles worshipped by the Graeco-Romans, but there is still plenty of fish*

Left: *solar boats were probably used in Khufu's funerary procession and then buried to be used in the Underworld*

MATHAF MARKIB EL-SHAMS (SOLAR BOAT MUSEUM) ✪✪✪

Five boat pits were discovered at the foot of the Pyramid of Khufu (▶ 17) and the 43m-long boat in the Solar Boat Museum was found in one of them. The boat, made of cedarwood, was in thousands of pieces, which took restorer Hagg Ahmed Yusuf fourteen years and a lot of patience to reconstruct. The result was worth it, for this simple boat is one of the most attractive of all Egyptian antiquities. Another boat, discovered in perfect condition in 1987, was left buried in the sand. The purpose of these boats remains unclear.

➕ 28C4
✉ Giza Plateau, 18km southwest of Cairo
🕐 Daily 9–4 (5 in summer)
🚌 Minibus 83
♿ Moderate
↔ Giza Pyramids and Sphinx (▶ 17)

MEMPHIS ✪✪

Little remains of the world's first imperial capital beyond a few statues and columns. King Menes is said to have united Egypt's southern valley and northern delta around 3100 BC and then created a new capital at Memphis, symbolically placed where delta and valley meet. Memphis became a magnificent city and for thousands of years was either Egypt's capital or second city. Most buildings in Memphis were constructed using mudbrick and have long since disappeared. The stone-built ones fared no better as they were quarried over the centuries to provide materials for monuments elsewhere. A small New Kingdom sphinx and a limestone colossus of Ramses II as a young man are on show in a modern pavilion in the open-air museum.

➕ 28C4
✉ Mit Rahina, 24km south of Cairo
🕐 Daily winter 7:30–4, summer 7:30–5
♿ Few
🖐 Moderate
↔ Saqqara (▶ 48)
❓ Public transport is difficult and it may be advisable to book a day trip to Memphis and Saqqara through a travel agent

🚩 29D4
✉ 5km north of centre of Cairo
🚇 Saray el-Qubba
🍴 Restaurants (££)

Below: *ancient Egyptians made pilgrimages to the Step Pyramid and considered its architect, Imhotep, a god*

🚩 28C4
✉ 2km west of Memphis
🕐 Daily 9–4
🍴 Café (£–££)
🚌 121 bus from Giza Pyramids to Badrasheen, then minibus to Saqqara village
▦ Moderate
↔ Memphis (➤ 47)
❓ The Step Pyramid can only be entered by special permit from the Egyptian Antiquities Inspectorate

MISR EL-GADIDA (HELIOPOLIS)

The city of the sun (On), which the Greeks calle Heliopolis, was one of ancient Egypt's most important c centres dedicated to the sun god Ra. Little has survived the city beyond an obelisk raised by Pharaoh Senusert but the modern suburb of Heliopolis is now a boomin district. It was planned at the end of the 19th century Belgian-born Baron Empain as a garden city. Empain eccentric villa, built like a Cambodian temple, now stan empty, but many grand villas and Moorish-style building along the elegant avenues are occupied, a testament to h vision. Amongst them, the former Heliopolis Palace Hot is now the official presidential residence.

SAQQARA ✪✪✪

Saqqara, the necropolis of the city of Memphis, is one the largest (7km long and 1.5km wide) and most importa cemeteries in Egypt, where much remains unexcavate The Old Kingdom royal family and nobles were burie here, and the cemetery was in use for more than 3,00 years. The Step Pyramid of King Djoser, part of the large funerary complex in Saqqara, was built by Djoser architect, Imhotep, in the 27th century BC. It was both th first pyramid in Egypt and at that time the large monument in the world built of hewn stone. The genius Imhotep, who was later deified for his efforts, was that started building a traditional *mastaba* (structure abov tombs) not in mudbrick but in stone, and then adde several more to create the six-step pyramid.

Visitors enter the funerary complex, originally enclosed by a limestone wall, from the rebuilt southeastern gate which leads to a Hypostyle Hall, and further on to the Great South Court. On the northern side of the pyramid stands the *serdab*, a box containing a replica of Djoser's life-size statue staring towards his immortality. Further northeast, next to the Pyramid of Teti, are two magnificent 6th-Dynasty *mastabas* of the Viziers Mereruka and Kagemni with the finest reliefs of the Old Kingdom. Next door, the *mastaba* of Ankh-ma-hor has particularly fine reliefs of craftsmen, and further west the *mastaba* of the Royal Hairdresser Ti has scenes from children's games. The Serapeum, the catacomb for the mummies of the sacred Apis bulls, has an eeriness to it. Walking back from the Serapeum towards the Step Pyramid, look for the *mastaba* of Akhti-Hotep and Ptah-Hotep which shows the various stages of the decoration of a tomb. South of Djoser's complex, the Pyramid of Unas contains a passageway leading to the burial chamber whose walls are decorated with the Pyramid texts, which are the earliest known example of decorative writing in a pharaonic tomb. The well-preserved *mastaba* of Queen Nebet, Unas's wife, has beautiful wall-paintings of the queen in the *harem* rooms of the palace, while the *mastaba* of Princess Idout gives an insight into the daily life of an Egyptian princess. Eastwards, the *mastaba* of Merou has splendid, very colourful scenes on the wall.

Exquisite wall carvings in the tomb of the priest Ptah-Hotep show a variety of offerings

49

Alexandria, the Northwest & the Oases

Alexandria was planned as Egypt's link to the Mediterranean world and still has a cosmopolitan air, in spite of the fact that most foreign inhabitants were forced out in the 1950s and 60s. Several other places in the northwest used to have foreign links but are now resolutely Egyptian: Mersa Matruh began as a trading post for Greeks and the northern Bedouin and in the mid-19th century Rashid (Rosetta) was popular with European residents.

The oases also had their distinct character. Cut off from the Nile valley and the coast by vast tracts of desert and visited regularly only by camel trains – the road to Siwa was only laid earlier this century – they have been bastions of tradition. But the advent of television, the Egyptian government's renewed interest and the growth of desert tourism is bringing sudden change.

> *'There is not much to see here, nothing but the perpetual feeling of being in the East, the eastern colouring, the eastern atmosphere.'*
>
> FLORENCE NIGHTINGALE
> from *Letters from Egypt*
> 19 November 1849

———————●———————

Wall-paintings evoking a pilgrimage to Mecca

Alexandria

Alexandria, Egypt's second largest city, was famous throughout the classical world as a place of learning and of academic achievement – its icon was the Pharos, a lighthouse, one of the seven wonders of the world. Centuries after its heyday, when conquered by the Arabs in AD 641, it was still described as a marble city of 4,000 palaces and 400 theatres. All that, like the tomb of Alexander the Great, is hidden somewhere underfoot. In the 19th century Alexandria grew rich from cotton and today it is an industrial city. Yet the past is always there, in reused ancient stones, in holes which suddenly appear in the road and reveal the hidden city, in the statues and blocks which cover the floor of its harbours and in the ambitions of its people.

Montazah Bay's private beach is cleaner and less crowded than most other beaches on the Alexandria coast

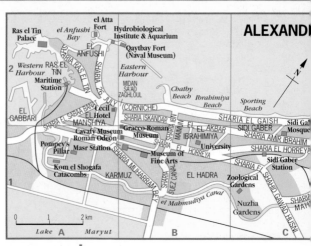

What to See in Alexandria

AMUD EL-SAWARI (POMPEY'S PILLAR)

Pompey's Pillar is one of Alexandria's famous landmarks, but ancient historians concentrate on the splendid monuments that surrounded it. The pink granite column, 27m high and 9m thick, was wrongly attributed to Pompey by the Crusaders: it was erected in honour of Diocletian CAD 295 and probably supported his equestrian statue. Long before the pillar was erected this hill was the citadel of Rhakotis, the settlement which Alexander the Great developed into Alexandria. Under the Ptolemies, a grand temple to Serapis, the Serapeum, flourished here and was a centre of world learning until destroyed by 4th-century Christians. When the great Alexandrian Library burned down, Cleopatra founded a new one at the Serapeum, donating her collection of some 200,000 manuscripts. The pillar and two Ptolemaic granite sphinxes on site and some remarkable statues in the Graeco-Roman Museum are all that remains of its glory.

KOM EL-DIKKA (ROMAN ODEON)

Alexandria's multi-layered history can be seen at Kom el-Dikka (Arabic for pile of rubble). Beneath late Roman ruins, 9th- and 10th-century Muslim tombs and a late 18th-century fort, archaeologists discovered an elegant 2nd-century AD amphitheatre with marble seating for 750 people. The mosaic flooring in the forecourt originally covered the whole area. Near by, a Graeco-Roman street disappears under modern Alexandria, and a residential area is still being uncovered, its houses and shops giving a glimpse of what life was like here thousands of years ago. Some finds from recent underwater excavations around the Pharos are also on display.

52A1
Sharia Amud el-Sawari, Karmuz
Daily 9–4
No 309 and 709 from Ramleh; tram 16 from Midan Saad Zaghloul
Cheap
Kom el-Shogafa Catacombs (► 54)

Above: *Alexandrians watched musical performances and wrestling contests at the pretty Roman theatre of Kom el-Dikka*

52A1
Behind Cinema Amir, off Sharia Salman Yusuf
03-490 2904
Daily 9–4
Cheap
Cavafy Museum (► 54), Graeco-Roman Museum (► 58)

53

<table>
<tr><td>

✚ 52A1
✉ Off Sharia Amud el-Sawari, Karmuz
🕐 Daily 9–4
💲 Moderate
↔ Pompey's Pillar (► 53)

Above: the tomb decorations at Kom el-Shogafa are typically Alexandrian with a surprising blend of Egyptian and classical elements

</td><td>

KOM EL-SHOGAFA CATACOMBS ✪✪✪

The catacombs at Kom el-Shogafa (Hill of Tiles) are unique both in plan and decoration, an unusual blend of ancient Egyptian, Greek and Roman designs which epitomised classical Alexandria's cosmopolitanism. The original 2nd century AD family vault was later enlarged to take in the community and thus created the largest Roman funerary complex found in Egypt.

The catacombs are on three levels, but the lowest floor is now inaccessible to visitors because of flooding. A wide staircase, lit by a central well through which corpses were lowered, leads through the first-floor vestibule to the Rotunda, where eight pillars support a domed roof, the Banquet Hall (to the left) and the Hall of Caracalla (to the right) with four painted tombs. A small spiral staircase leads to the eerie second-level tombs, which have wonderful decorations of bearded serpents, Medusas, a falcon Horus and the Egyptian gods Anubis and Sobek dressed as Roman soldiers.

</td></tr>
</table>

✚ 52A1
✉ 4 Sharia Sharm el-Sheikh, off Sharia Sultan Hussein
🕐 Daily 9–2, also 6–8PM on Tue, Thu. Closed Mon
💲 Free
↔ Kom el-Dikka (► 53), Graeco-Roman Museum (► 58)

MATHAF CAVAFY (CAVAFY MUSEUM) ✪

The apartment where the famous Greek poet Constantine Cavafy (1863–1933) lived for the last 25 years of his life has become a museum. 'Where could I live better?' he said. 'Below, the brothel caters for the flesh. And there is the church which forgives sin. And there is the hospital where we die.' His furniture, icons, death mask, books and the desk at which he wrote some of his greatest poetry, including *The City* and *The Barbarians,* can be seen.

Walk in Downtown Alexandria

Start at the Cecil Hotel. Turn left down the Corniche and continue to the Tomb of the Unknown Soldier, then turn left again.

This is the heart of the old European Alexandria, marked by an equestrian statue of Muhammad Ali.

At Midan el Tahrir turn left along Sharia Salah Salem.

Note the Moorish Anglican Church of St Mark and the National Bank of Egypt, a copy of Palazzo Farnese in Rome.

Continue along Sharia Fouad and at Patisserie Venous turn right into Sharia Nabi Danyal.

Half-way up the street, on the left, is Nabi Danyal Mosque built over a cistern, which until recently was believed to contain Alexander the Great's tomb.

Turn left into Sharia Yussef with the Roman Odeon (➤ 53) on your left. After a visit continue along the same street and turn left round the site of the theatre.

Stop for lunch at Pastroudis, the famous patisserie.

Cross the road into Sharia Zangalola.

This leads to the Greek Orthodox Church of St Saba.

Follow the street to the left of the church and then turn into the first street to the right, Sharia Sharm el-Sheikh. The Cavafy Museum is at No 4 (➤ 54). Walk left out of the museum, turn left onto Sharia Sultan Hussein, and then right into Sharia Nabi Danyal.

You will pass the Coptic Cathedral of St Mark (on the left) and Alexandria's neo-classical synagogue (on the right).

Continue along the street back to the Cecil.

Distance
2½km

Time
2½ hours without visits, 4 hours with visits

Start/End Point
Midan Sa'ad Zaghloul
➕ 52B2

Lunch
Pastroudis (£–££)
✉ 39 Sharia el Hurriya
☎ 03-492 9609

Pastroudis was a haunt of the poet Cavafy and some of the characters in Lawrence Durrell's The Alexandria Quartet

Food & Drink

Few people travel to Egypt just to eat, because although many local dishes are delicious, the cuisine is basic and the best of it is prepared at home.

A table full of mezze including dips, salads, olives and pickles is more than a meal in itself

In restaurants, Egyptians often share a number of *mezze* (appetisers) to accompany drinks or as starters before a grill. Wall-paintings in ancient Egyptian tombs show large banquets with mounds of food and the pharaohs' descendants continue this tradition; both at home and in restaurants huge amounts of food usually arrive to dazzle the appetite. Popular *mezze* include *wara'a aynab* (stuffed vine leaves), *tahina* (sesame paste), *baba ghanoug* (puréed aubergine with *tahina*), *hummus* (chickpea purée) and salads. *Bladi*, similar to pitta bread, is often used instead of a fork to scoop up the food.

National Dishes

Egyptian food has Syrian, Lebanese and Turkish influences. Stewed *fuul* or fava beans (➤ 99), drizzled with oil, spiced with chilli, cumin and lemon juice are eaten for breakfast or as a snack during the day. *Fuul* often comes with more beans, this time mashed, rolled into balls and fried, called *taamiya*. Vegetarians or carbohydrate fanatics love *kushari*, a mixture of macaroni, rice, fried onions, chickpeas and lentils, topped with a spicy tomato sauce and eaten any time of the day. Slightly more up-market is *meloukhiya*, a spinach-like vegetable made into a thick soup with garlic, rabbit or chicken. Chicken and red meat are usually grilled, most often as kebab (lamb or beef skewers) or *kofta* (meatballs). Pigeon (*hamama*) is a delicacy, especially stuffed with wheat.

Egyptian patisseries sell an endless variety of sweets, candied fruits, chocolates and pastries

Sweets

The most popular oriental pastries are *basbousa* (oven-baked semolina cake soaked in honey), *baklawa* (filo pastry stuffed with nuts and honey) and *kunafa* (angelhair stuffed either with thick cream, cream cheese or nuts). The best of Egyptian desserts is *Umm Ali*, a rich mixture of cracker bread, coconut, cream, nuts and raisins, soaked in hot milk. *Roz bi-laban* (rice pudding), *mahallabiya* (cornflour pudding) and *crème caramel* are standards on restaurant menus.

It is often more refreshing to drink a good cup of sweet mint tea than an icy cold drink

Café Pleasures

Tea is a good thirst quencher, even in the heat, and Turkish coffee with sugar (*qahwa mazbout*) soon becomes a habit, but cafés have other pleasures to offer. All year round there are fresh fruit juices (▶ 94), as well a wide selection of soft drinks. Egyptians claim that 'once you drink from the Nile you will always come back', but it is wiser to stick to bottled mineral water. Traditional cafés also serve herbal infusions such as *yansoon* (anis), *helba* (fenugreek), *karkadeh* (hibiscus) and *'irfa* (cinnamon), and in winter try *sahlab*, a creamy concoction of arrowroot and cinnamon, usually topped with nuts and coconut.

Alcoholic Drinks

Although most Egyptians, as Muslims, do not drink alcohol, it is usually available wherever tourism is well established. Locally brewed Stella beers are very drinkable and some imported beers are also available. In spite of its pharaonic tradition, Egyptian wine is variable in quality and often best avoided. Most imported wines are sold at inflated prices, even in tax-free shops. Avoid local impersonations of famous-brand spirits – Johnny Talker, Marcel Horse and Ricardo – which are disgusting.

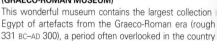

52B1

5 Sharia el-Mathaf

03-482 6434

Daily 9–4, Fri 9–11:30, 1:30–4

Café (£)

Cheap

Kom el-Dikka (➤ 53), Cavafy Museum (➤ 54)

MATHAF GRAECO-ROMAN (GRAECO-ROMAN MUSEUM)

😊😊😊

This wonderful museum contains the largest collection Egypt of artefacts from the Graeco-Roman era (rough 331 BC–AD 300), a period often overlooked in the country other museums. Most of the 40,000 exhibits were four in and around Alexandria; a few, especially the intrigui funerary masks (rooms 7, 8 and 10) and the amazir mummified crocodile (room 9) came from el-Fayour (➤ 46). Highlights of the museum include the splend

2nd-century AD black-granit Apis bull and the statue of Serapis (room 6) from th Serapeum (➤ 53). Serapis, th main god of Alexandria, was hybrid of the Greek go Dionysos and, through the Ap bull, the Egyptian god Osiri Rooms 16–16a have som exquisite Hellenistic sculpture including an elegant Aphrodit and some vivid torsos, bu perhaps the most pleasing the eye is the museum' wonderful collection of lifelik terracotta *Tanagra* (room 18a placed in the tombs of wome and children as a celebration youth and beauty. Rooms 1– are devoted to Coptic art fro the Monastery of Abu Min 50km west of Alexandri which was once the mos popular place of pilgrimage the east. The garden contain more sculpture and some roc cut tombs.

52C1

21 Sharia Ahmed Yehia, Glim, behind the governor's residence

03-586 8348

Daily 9–4, Fri 9–11:30, 1:30–4

Tramline No 2 from Ramleh to Qasr el-Safa

Moderate

MATHAF EL-MUGAWHARAT (ROYAL JEWELLERY MUSEUM)

😊😊

This splendid little museum is housed in the slightly kitso neo-classical palace of Princess Fatma el-Zahraa, a gran daughter of Ibrahim Pasha. The palace, with its staine glass windows portraying events in European history, i cherubs and paintings, is worth a visit in itself. The roy jewellery collection dates from the time of Muhammad A to the abdication of King Farouk in 1952. Everythir sparkles as precious stones are set into every possibl object, including Muhammad Ali's enamelled snuff box, a platinum crown inset with 2,159 diamonds, ashtrays, gold knobs inlaid with diamonds, and a gold and silver chess board. All exhibits are well labelled in Arabic and English.

QASR EL-MUNTAZAH (MUNTAZAH PALACE) ✪✪

Khedive Abbas II's extravagant Turko-Florentine palace, now the presidential summer residence, is closed to the public, but the vast, beautiful gardens are a popular day trip for Alexandrian families, despite the spread of fast-food outlets. Muntazah beach, near the Palestine Hotel (➤ 102), is one of the most pleasant near Alexandria, separated from Ma'amoura by a pretty Turkish-style belvedere.

✚ 52C1
✉ Muntazah Bay
🍴 Fast food restaurants (£), restaurants at Palestine and Salamlek hotels (£££)
🚌 Bus 260 from Ramleh to Abu Qir
♿ Few
💲 Cheap

QASR QAYTBAY (QAYTBAY FORT) ✪✪

The fabled lighthouse or Pharos of Alexandria, one of the ancient world's seven wonders, was built in 279 BC by Sostratus for Ptolemy II. It was reputedly over 125m high and had more than 300 rooms for the staff who worked in it. It was destroyed by earthquakes in the 11th and 14th centuries, but recent underwater excavations have revealed several fragments of it. In 1479 Sultan Qaytbay built his fort on the site, reusing some of the Pharos's stones and columns, notably in the west-facing outer wall. The fort is now used as a Naval Museum, which is of little interest to the average visitor, although the views from the walls are magnificent.

✚ 52B2
✉ End of the Corniche
☎ 03-809 144
🕐 Daily 9–4, Fri 9–11:30, 1:30–4, Naval Museum 9–3 except Fri
🚌 Minibus No 706 or 707 from Midan Orabi or No 15 tram from Ramleh
💲 Cheap
↪ Near by is Alexandria's lively fish market and aquarium

Opposite: *Ptolemy I introduced the cult of Serapis – the god's shape came to him in a dream*

Left: *the Egyptian flag flies from the top of the 15th-century Qaytbay fort*

What to See in the Northwest

EL-ALAMEIN

Winston Churchill wrote: 'Before Alamein we never had a victory. After Alamein we never had a defeat.' The 194 battle between the German Afrika Korps and the Allie Eighth Army at el-Alamein marked a turning point in Wor War II. Around 11,000 soldiers were killed, many of the are buried in the town's cemeteries. The War Museu illustrates with maps, uniforms and models the Nor Africa Campaign as well as the 1973 war between Egy and Israel.

MERSA MATRUH

Mersa Matruh has grown from a sleepy fishing town into sprawling, dull summer resort for Egyptian holidaymaker In the summer the once superb beaches are no overcrowded and full of litter, and Western women ma feel awkward bathing amongst fully clothed Egyptia women. Rommel's Beach, where the Desert Fc reputedly went for a swim, is slightly cleaner but the be beaches are some way west of town: Cleopatra's Beac (7km), El-Obeid Beach (20km) and the splendid Agiba Beach (28km) with deep turquoise water. The Romm Museum, in a cave behind the port, has a collection Rommel's memorabilia, including his maps and coat.

RASHID (ROSETTA)

Rosetta's surviving mansions are proof that this rath neglected town knew better days: during the Ottoman er it was a larger port than Alexandria. The 18th-century Ba Arab Kily house on Midan Gumhuriya, now Rosetta Museum, is typical, built in Delta-style architecture wi red and black brickwork and fine woodwork. The gran early 19th-century Bayt el-Amasyali has some stunnir inlay work and painted ceilings. The roof of the 17t

+ 28B5
- 106km west of Alexandria
- Museum daily 8–6, Commonwealth War Cemetery daily 7–4:30
- Alamein Rest House (£) ☎ 03-430 2785
- Buses from Alexandria to Mersa Matruh stop 200m from the War Museum, but no transport to the cemeteries
- Few
- Museum cheap, cemeteries free

Anti-aircraft guns abandoned in the desert during World War II in the open-air section of el-Alamein's Military Museum

+ 28B5
- 290km from Alexandria, 512km from Cairo
- Governate House
- Beau Site Hotel/ Restaurant (££) on Sharia el-Shati ☎ 03-933 319
- Buses from Cairo and Alexandria
- Domestic flights from Cairo
- Few

+ 28C5
- 64km east of Alexandria
- Museum daily 8–2, fort daily 9–4
- Cafés (£) on main street
- Hourly bus from Alexandria, Midan el-Gumhuriya
- Cheap

century Zaghloul Mosque has collapsed, so what is left is an eerie garden of about 300 columns partly submerged in a murky pool of water. Five kilometres north of the town, Qaytbay's 15th-century fort marks the end of the Nile's 5,440km-long run from East Africa into the Mediterranean. Near here, in 1799, a French officer discovered a 2nd-century BC basalt stone with inscriptions in three scripts, hieroglyphs, demotic and Greek. It was from this Rosetta Stone, now in London's British Museum, that French scholar Jean François Champollion deciphered ancient Egyptian hieroglyphs.

A wonderful fresco of the Annunciation in the Church of el-Adhra (the Virgin) at Deir el-Suryani

WADI EL-NATRUN 😊😊

Although monasticism started in the Eastern Desert (► 87), it was in Wadi Natrun that the rules were developed. For the last 1,500 years the Coptic popes have been chosen from these monasteries. The current pope, Shenuda III, formerly a monk at Deir el-Suryani, has encouraged a monastic revival – many monks are now multilingual and highly educated. St Bishoi (AD 320–407) was one of the earliest monks in Wadi Natrun and his monastery still has more than 100 monks and several hermits. Deir el-Suryani was founded in the 6th-century by displeased monks from Deir Bishoi and later taken over by Syrian monks. Deir el-Suryani's Church of the Virgin has some magnificent frescoes and also the cave where St Bishoi prayed with his hair tied to the ceiling to keep him upright. The oldest and most remote of these monasteries is Deir Baramus, founded by two sons of Emperor Valentine who died during their fasting. Deir el-Maqar was founded by St Makarius, who died in AD 390 after spending 60 years as a hermit in the desert.

🚹 28C5
✉ 105km from Cairo, off Alexandria Desert Road
🕐 Check with Coptic Patriarchate ☎ 02-282 5374/284 3159 for opening times. Deir Anba Bishoi is open daily, Deir el-Maqar is closed to the public
🍴 Wadi Natrun Resthouse (£–££) on Desert Road
🚌 Buses between Cairo and Alexandria to the Resthouse, and from there regular pick-ups to the monasteries
💰 Donations appreciated
❓ Monasteries are closed during the five seasons of Fast (dates variable)

The Western Desert Oases

The Western Desert, covering some 3 millio sq km, runs from the Mediterranean south t Kordofan in Central Sudan, and from the Ni Valley west to Fezzan in Libya.

What to See in the Oases

BAHARIYA

On the main street of Bahar</br>iya's main town, el-Bawiti, the Oasis Heritage Museum, with exhibits on Bedouin li and a little shop selling excellent local crafts. In the midd of the gardens (used to cultivate fruit trees) are the Roma el-Bishnu springs; however, these are not recommende for bathing. Instead, take a day trip to some of the dese springs or spend a night in the amazing White Desert e route to Farafra. Further along the oasis road is el-Qas built over Bahariya's ancient capital, with the remains of Temple of Bes (664–525 BC) and a Roman Triumphal Arch

DAKHLA

Mut, the ancient and modern capital, has a sma Ethnographic Museum, with scenes of life in the oase and hot springs believed to cure colds and rheumatism. A Qasr, about 30km from Mut, is Dakhla's medieval capit of three-storey mudbrick houses. The Ayyubid Nasr el-D Mosque is notable for its 21m-high wooden minaret. Fiv kilometres further west are the beautifully decorated 1 and 2nd-century AD Muwazaka Tombs and 2km fror there, the 1st-century AD Roman temple of Deir el-Haggar

FARAFRA

Qasr Farafra is the only settlement in this most beautif oasis, with a small, pretty mudbrick museum built by loc artist Badr. Walking in the peaceful palm groves and love gardens make up for a lack of ancient monuments.

+ 28B4
✉ 360km from Cairo
🍴 Cafés/restaurant (£)
🚌 Daily buses from Cairo el-Azhar bus station. Buses to Farafra on Sat, Mon, Thu between 1 and 2PM

Above: *farming in the fields of the oases is a labour-intensive job*

+ 28B2
✉ 310km from Farafra
ℹ For information
☎ 088-940 407
🍴 Cafés (£)
🚌 Daily buses from Cairo, Asyut, Kharga, Farafra, Bahariya
🎟 Sights cheap

+ 28B3
✉ 180km from el-Bawiti, Bahariya
🍴 A few restaurants (£)
🚌 Daily buses from Cairo, Bahariya and Dakhla, except on Wed
❓ Tours to the White Desert from Saad Café

DID YOU KNOW?

Once rather remote and rarely visited, the Western Deser oases have recently became more accessible with the opening of a new railway from Safaga, on the Red Sea coast, to Kharga and Baris. There are plans to link it up with the Toshka region further south, where Egyptians are working on the ambitious Toshka canal project, designed to irrigate the desert in the 21st century.

KHARGA ⭐⭐

Modern Kharga town has borne the brunt of the government's New Valley development and has little charm, although the El-Wadi el-Gadid Museum is worth visiting to see well-labelled displays of locally found artefacts. North of the town, beyond the ruined Ptolemaic temple of Nadura, stands one of Egypt's few surviving Persian monuments, the 6th-century BC Temple of Hibis dedicated to Amun-Re. Near by is the impressive Bagawat necropolis with finely decorated Christian chapels from the 3rd to the 7th centuries AD. North of the necropolis, and only accessible by car, are two superb Roman fortresses and some remarkable aqueducts.

- 28C2
- ✉ 195km from Dakhla
- ℹ Sharia Nasser ☎ 092-901 611
- 🕐 Museum daily 8–4; Bagawat necropolis daily 8–6 summer, 8–5 winter
- 🍴 Hotel restaurants (£–££)
- 🚌 Daily buses from Cairo, Asyut, and other oases
- 🚆 Trains from Baris, Qena and Safaga
- ✈ Two flights a week from Cairo

SIWA ⭐⭐⭐

A new road has ended Siwa's legendary isolation, but in spite of dramatic changes, it is still a sleepy and relaxed town. The Traditional Siwan House shows what most Siwan houses looked like before breezeblock arrived. The new town lies in the shadow of abandoned Shali, the mudbrick hilltop town founded in 1203 and fortified against Bedouin attacks, which is floodlit at night. Alexander the Great came to Siwa in 331 BC to consult the Oracle at the ancient settlement of Aghurmi, 3km east of the modern town. The 26th Dynasty Temple of the Oracle dedicated to Amun-Re has survived well. From the minaret of Aghurmi's Mosque there are excellent views of this picturesque settlement, inhabited until the early 20th century, and over towards the nearby temple of Umm Ubayda. The salt lake Birket Siwa and Fantis Island are a favourite picnic spot and a good place to swim. Siwans are traditional people and visitors should show them respect by dressing modestly, and abstaining from alcohol and from public displays of affection.

- 28A4
- ✉ 300km south of Mersa Matruh
- ℹ Near new mosque ☎ 03-934026 ext 6131
- 🍴 Cafés/restaurants (£–££)
- 🚌 2 daily buses from Mersa Matruh and Alexandria
- ❓ Siwa Festival 3 days in October just before the date harvest; Traditional Siwan House Museum is open 10–12 noon on request – ask the day before; Fri market

Above: *a blue version of a pilgrim's trip by boat to Mecca from the oasis of Siwa*

63

Nile Valley &
Lake Nasser

In a land with little rain, ancient Egyptians recognised that the Nile's annual summer flooding was a blessing, and so organised themselves to make the most of the flood and the fertile silt it left as it receded. In the process they created the model for society as we know it; a hierarchy of workers, administrators and higher management (pharaohs) that also made possible the construction of huge temples and tombs. The annual flooding created seasons of field work and enforced rest, which characterised life in the Egyptian countryside until the end of the 19th century. The completion of the two Aswan dams (1902 and 1971), which lost Nubia beneath Lake Nasser, ended that annual cycle of drought and flood. In spite of the many changes that have followed, the Nile remains as much Egypt's lifeline as it was in the past.

> *'...anyone who sees Egypt,*
> *without having heard a word*
> *about it before, must*
> *perceive... that the Egypt to*
> *which the Greeks go in their*
> *ships is an acquired country,*
> *the gift of the river...'*

HERODOTUS
The Histories
*c*460 BC

Ramses II at Luxor Temple, staring into eternity

Luxor

Luxor is built over part of ancient Thebes, also known as Uast or Apet. One of the great cities of the ancient world, Thebes spread across both sides of the Nile and was the political capital of Egypt during the Middle and New Kingdoms. Some of the most famous pharaohs – Ramses II, Seti I, Hatshepsut, Tutankhamun – lived here and left their mark. Long after political power passed to the north, Theban temples remained the centre of religious influence thanks to huge gifts of land, gold and revenues, particularly to Amun's main temple at Karnak. The glory of Thebes was still very real when the Greek poet Homer wrote about its 100 gates, but the 6th-century BC Persian King Cambyses hastened its long decline by setting fire to everything that could be burned. Most of what has survived that and the ravages of centuries are the remains of stone temples and rock-cut tombs.

The Temple of Luxor, right in the heart of the modern town, is difficult to miss

Early Christians defaced many temple images and converted some of the courts into churches, while Arab Muslims, whose religion banned the representation of people, generally showed no interest in the ruins. Difficulties of Nile travel for foreigners gave Thebes and the rest of the Upper Nile valley a legendary status in the West. Its rediscovery, starting in earnest in the 18th century and continuing today (KV5, the largest tomb so far found in Egypt, is still being excavated in the Valley of the Kings) has attracted many visitors from around the world. As a result, Luxor has grown from a village in the 1860s to become a small town in 1895, and today is a busy modern city.

What to See on the East Bank

KARNAK (► 20–1, TOP TEN)

MAB'AD EL-UQSUR (LUXOR TEMPLE) ✪✪✪

The Temple of Luxor or the 'harem of the south', like nearby Karnak, is dedicated to the Theban triad of Amun-Min, Mut and Khonsu, but it is a far more coherent building as fewer pharaohs added to the temple complex. During the Opet (fertility) festival, a procession of holy barges brought Amun's statue from Karnak to Luxor, where he was united with his wife Mut to ensure an excellent harvest. The mosque built over part of the temple is dedicated to Luxor's patron saint Abu el-Haggag, during whose moulid (► 116) feluccas are pulled around the temple, perhaps a reminder of the ancient festival.

The First Pylon, built by Ramses II, features his favourite theme of victory at the battle of Kadesh. His two colossi, a ruined standing statue and one of two splendid obelisks (the other one now adorns the Place de la Concorde in Paris) flank the entrance. In the Court of Ramses II there is an interesting relief of the temple itself and, to the right, a funerary procession led by Ramses II's many sons. Beyond the Second Pylon the impressive Colonnade of Amenophis III leads to the wide Court of Amenophis III and a small Hypostyle Hall. The inner sanctum contains a number of shrines, including a columned portico used as a chapel by Roman soldiers, Alexander the Great's Sanctuary of the Sacred Barge and to the left Amenophis III's Birth Room, near which the cache of statues now on view in the Luxor Museum (► 68) were found.

✚ 29D2

✉ Corniche, East Bank

⏰ Daily 7AM–10PM in summer, 7AM–9PM in winter (best explored in daylight, but try to return at night when spotlights add to the atmosphere and accentuate the carvings)

▦ Moderate

↔ Karnak (► 20), Mummification Museum (► 68)

❓ Son et lumière shows every evening at 6, 7:15, 8:30, and 9:45 on weekends

Above: verticle grooves along the pylon façade of Luxor Temple supported flagpoles, while the openings above them were for the braces holding the poles

67

🚻 29D2
✉ Corniche, East Bank
🕐 9–1, 5–10 (4–9 in winter)
♿ Few
🍴 Moderate
↔ Karnak (➤ 20–1), Luxor
Temple (➤ 67), Luxor
Museum (➤ below)

🚻 29D2
✉ Corniche, East Bank
🕐 Daily 9–1, 5–10 in
summer, 9–1, 4–9 in
winter
♿ Few
🍴 Expensive; additional
ticket (cheap) for New
Hall
↔ Karnak (➤ 20–1), Luxor
Temple (➤ 67),
Mummification Museum
(➤ above)

*Egyptian art students
sketching some of the
well-displayed collection
of antiquities at the
Luxor Museum*

MATHAF EL-MUMMIA
(MUMMIFICATION MUSEUM) ⭐

Luxor's newest museum (also ➤ 111), the first of its kin in the world, houses a unique collection of mummie including mummified animals such as cats, fish and croc diles, as well as tools used for mummification. Everythin is well displayed and labelled, giving a clear insight into th whole mummification process.

MATHAF EL-UQSUR LI-L-ATHAAR
(LUXOR MUSEUM) ⭐⭐⭐

This small modern museum is one of the finest in Egy and most exhibits are from local temples and tombs. Wh sets it apart is that displays are carefully chosen, we labelled and perfectly lit, to make the most of their beaut Much of the ground floor is dedicated to New Kingdo statues, including a superb bust of the young Tuthmosis (No 61) and a bizarre alabaster statue of the crocodile g Sobek holding Amenophis III (No 107).

The upper floor has a beautiful mural from Akhenaton temple at Karnak, with the king and his wife worshippin the sun god Aton. A glass case shows some objects fro Tutankhamun's tomb in the Valley of the Kings (➤ 1 including two fine model boats, a superb gold-inlaid cow head, sandals and arrows. The New Hall displays th cache of 26 statues found in 1989, near Amenophis II Birth Room in Luxor Temple.

What to See on the West Bank

BIBAN EL-HARIM (VALLEY OF THE QUEENS) ★★

Known in ancient times as the 'place of beauty', this was the resting place of more than 80 queens and princes from the 18th to the 20th Dynasties (1570–1070 BC), many of whom have not been identified. The tombs are far less grand and elaborate than those in the Valley of the Kings, and many were left unfinished, suggesting that queens and their offspring were considerably less important than the pharaohs themselves. The tomb of Nefertari, the wife of Ramses II, is the exception, and its exquisite paintings have been restored. Several sons of Ramses III died young of smallpox and, unusually, the reliefs in their tombs show them being led by their father through the underworld.

✚ 69A2
✉ 3km south of the Valley of the Nobles, West Bank
🕐 Daily 7–6 in summer, 7–5 in winter
🎟 Tickets for Nefertari's tomb are limited to 200 a day, and cost LE100; the other three tombs open to the public are moderate
↔ Deir el-Medina (➤ 70)
❓ Some tombs may be closed for restoration

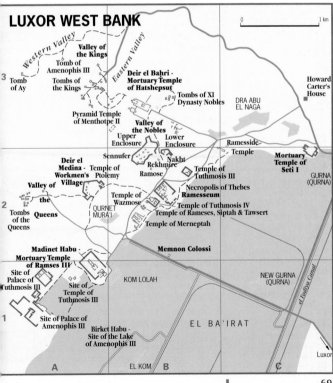

LUXOR WEST BANK

0 _____ 1 km

Western Valley

Valley of the Kings
Tomb of Amenophis III
Eastern Valley

3 Tomb of Ay
Tombs of the Kings

Deir el Bahri - Mortuary Temple of Hatshepsut

Tombs of XI Dynasty Nobles

DRA ABU EL NAGA

Howard Carter's House

Pyramid Temple of Menthotpe II

Valley of the Nobles
Upper Enclosure
Lower Enclosure

Sennufer
Rekhmire
Nakht
Ramose

Rameside Temple

Mortuary Temple of Seti I

Deir el Medina - Workmen's Village

Temple of Ptolemy

Temple of Tuthmosis III

GURNA (QURNA)

Valley of the Queens

Necropolis of Thebes

Temple of Wazmose

QURNET MURA'I

Ramesseum

Temple of Tuthmosis IV
Temple of Rameses, Siptah & Tawsert

2 Tombs of the Queens

Temple of Merneptah

Madinet Habu - Mortuary Temple of Ramses III

Memnon Colossi

Site of Palace of Tuthmosis III

Site of Temple of Tuthmosis III

KOM LOLAH

NEW GURNA (QURNA)

el Fadiya Canal

1 Site of Palace of Amenophis III

Birket Habu - Site of the Lake of Amenophis III

EL BA'IRAT

Luxor

A   B   C

EL KOM

69B3

West Bank

Daily 7–6 in summer, 7–5 in winter

Café (£)

Tickets must be bought at the central ticket office (on the river bank), and are sold per group of tombs: moderate

Ramesseum (► 73), Deir el-Bahri (► below)

Check at ticket office which tombs are open, as some may be closed for a while to protect them from mass tourism

69B3

West Bank

7–6 in summer, 7–5 in winter

Drinks (£)

Moderate

Ramesseum (► 73), Valley of the Nobles (► above)

It is possible to walk over the hill, or take a donkey, to the Valley of the Kings (► 18) with fantastic views over Luxor and the monuments

Opposite: *relief showing the falcon-headed sun god in the mortuary temple of Hatshepsut*

69A2

West Bank

7–6 in summer, 7–5 in winter

Café (£)

Moderate

Ramesseum (► 73), Madinat Habu (► 72), Valley of the Queens (► 69)

Only two tombs are open

70

BIBAN EL-MULUK (VALLEY OF THE KINGS) (► 18, TOP TEN)

BIBAN EL-NUBALAA (VALLEY OF THE NOBLES)

Whilst the pharaohs' tombs were decorated with religio texts, those of the nobles depict the good life they had l on earth in the hope that it would continue after th death. The result is often more satisfying than the ro tombs. It is easy to imagine these peoples' lives a interests, because their tombs show scenes of family li agriculture, and how they imagined the afterlife, includi the boat journey to Abydos and funerary banquets. As t quality of limestone was too poor for carvings, the scenes were painted on plaster. Three pairs of tombs a particularly worth visiting for their amazing and we preserved paintings: Nakht and Menna; Rekhmire a Sennofer; Ramose, Userhat and Khaemhat.

DEIR EL-BAHRI (MORTUARY TEMPLE OF HATSHEPSUT)

Dramatically set against the Theban hills, this splen temple built by Queen Hatshepsut's architect (and perha also her lover) Senenmut, always surprises by its simplic and almost modern look. Queen Hatshepsut was the o female pharaoh to reign over Egypt, taking power from h stepson, Tuthmosis III, when her husband Tuthmosis died. The temple terraces were filled with exotic trees a fountains, and linked to the Nile by an avenue of Sphinx The colonnades of the Lower Terrace were defaced Tuthmosis III, but the Middle Terrace colonnades are fas nating. To the right is the Birth Colonnade, confirming t Queen's divine parentage. On the left is the Pu Colonnade, depicting a journey to Punt (probably in toda Somalia) where expeditions were sent to bring back my trees, ebony, ivory and spices. Beyond lies the Chapel Hathor with bovine Hathor columns.

DEIR EL-MEDINA (WORKERS' VILLAGE)

Artists and artisans worked on tombs in the Valley of Kings (► 18) for ten days at a time before returning their family home in Deir el-Medina, where they built th own tombs. The tomb of Sennedjem has very fine w paintings of agricultural scenes, Sennedjem and his wife front of the gods, and a depiction of the tree of life fr which a goddess appears. The tomb of Ankherha is equa brightly painted with scenes of Ankherha's family with l of children.

69C2

✉ Gurna, West Bank

🕐 7–6 in summer, 7–5 in winter

🚹 Moderate

↔ Deir el-Bahri (➤ 70)

69A2

✉ Kom Lolah, West Bank

🕐 7–6 in summer, 7–5 in winter

🍴 Outside the gates two cafés serve lunch (£)

🚹 Moderate

↔ Deir el-Medina (➤ 70), Memnon Colossi (➤ 73)

Below: *the well-preserved temple of Madinet Habu is one of the easiest temples to understand as there were very few additions to the original plan*

MAB'AD SETI (TEMPLE OF SETI I) ✪✪

Dedicated to the god Amun and to Seti's father Ramses this largely destroyed temple still shows the hallmark Seti I (1291–1278 BC) with some of the wall decoratio and reliefs of the New Kingdom. The first two pylons a courts have disappeared and today only the temple prop remains. A colonnade leads into a Hypostyle Hall wi columns decorated with reliefs of Seti I and Ramse making offerings to the gods. The chapel to the left of t temple's main entrance is dedicated to Ramses I, w died before a temple could be built for him.

MADINET HABU ✪✪✪
(MORTUARY TEMPLE OF RAMSES III)

Ramses III (1182–1151 BC) modelled this impressi temple on his forefather Ramses II's mortuary temp (Ramesseum, ➤ opposite). Madinat Habu is not on ma tourists' itinerary, even though it was the last classi pharaonic temple built, with very few later additions. T vast temple complex is entered through a high gatehous built as a Syrian-style fortress, and the steps lead to pharaoh's pleasure apartments with a good view over t grounds. The magnificent First Pylon records battles th Ramses III never fought, most likely copied from Rams II's temple. The First and Second Courts are vast and lin with images of Ramses III making offerings to the go but the Hypostyle Hall and Inner Sanctuaries were sever damaged during an earthquake in 27 BC. After visiting t temple walk along the outer walls, decorated with m giant reliefs of Ramses III fishing, hunting or at war. On south side are the ruins of Ramses III's palace.

MEMNON COLOSSI ✪✪

Amenophis III's (1386–1349 BC) giant colossi stare peacefully over green fields, unconcerned that their faces as well as the mortuary temple they once guarded, disappeared long ago. The right-hand statue cracked during an earthquake in 27 BC, and subsequently groaned each dawn and dusk, which the Greeks interpreted as Memnon singing to his mother Eos, the dawn goddess. Even though the groaning stopped when Emperor Septimus Severus had the statue repaired in AD 199, the colossi have been a tourist attraction ever since. Smaller statues of Queen Tiy and Amenophis III's mother, Mutemuia, flank the pharaoh's legs, while the sides of the seats are decorated with sunken reliefs of round-bellied Nile gods with papyrus and lotus, the flowers of Upper and Lower Egypt.

🔢 69B2
✉ On the side of the main road to the ticket office, West Bank
🕐 7–6 in summer, 7–5 in winter
🖐 Free
↔ Deir el-Medina (➤ 70), Madinat Habu (➤ 72)

Below: *the head of the statue of Ramses II ruined part of the Ramesseum when it fell*

RAMESSEUM ✪✪

Ramses II (1279–1212 BC) built magnificent temples, including large parts of Karnak (➤ 20–1) and Luxor Temple (➤ 67) and two temples at Abu Simbel, but he did not do well with his own mortuary temple. Although it must have rivalled the others for beauty, it fell because it was built on weak foundations. The temple entrance now leads to the First Pylon, decorated with scenes from the Battle at Kadesh. On the south side of the First Courtyard are the remains of the Palace where Ramses II stayed during religious festivals. At the other end, near the Second Pylon, is the base of the statue of 'Ozymandias' (a Greek misreading of one of Ramses's titles), which inspired the British poet Shelley. Once the largest statue in the world, weighing over 900 tonnes, it ruined the Second Court when it fell. The head and part of the torso remain, poignantly, where they landed; other parts of the statue are now in museums all over the world. The Hypostyle Hall is decorated with battle scenes, and the ceiling of the Astronomic Room is painted with the oldest known 12-month calendar.

🔢 69B2
✉ Opposite the Tombs of the Nobles, West Bank
🕐 7–6 in summer, 7–5 in winter
🖐 Moderate
↔ Valley of the Nobles (➤ 70), Deir el-Medina (➤ 70)

What to See in Central Nile Valley

This area may be subject to security alerts (➤ 122, Personal Safety).

ABYDOS (➤ 16, TOP TEN)

BENI HASAN ●●

Beni Hasan is a Middle Kingdom necropolis on the east bank of the river, with four tombs open to the public. They belonged to local governors and are remarkable for their elegant columns and fine paintings on stucco. These depict scenes from daily life, agriculture and hunting, as well as more unusual acrobats and wrestlers.

DANDARA, TEMPLE OF HATHOR ●●●

The beautiful Temple of Hathor was built between 125 BC and AD 60 as part of an attempt by the Ptolemies and the Romans to reinforce their position by claiming association with the ancient Egyptian gods. There was probably an earlier temple of Hathor here, as this was the site where Hathor was believed to have given birth to Horus's son. During the New Year festival, Hathor's statue was taken in procession to the roof, where it was exposed to the sun god Re before being escorted to the temple at Edfu (➤ 80) to be reunited with Horus. Scenes of this festival decorate the temple walls, as well as reliefs of Roman emperors performing ancient Egyptian rituals. The carvings are much cruder than earlier pharaonic work, but the temple has been well-preserved and remains impressive.

✚ 28C3
✉ 20km south of el-Minya
🕐 Daily 7–5
🚌 Bus or service taxi to Abu Qirkus from Minya, then ferry across to the site
✋ Cheap

✚ 29D3
✉ 4km across the Nile from Qena, 64km north of Luxor
🕐 Daily 7–6
🍴 Café (£)
🚌 Taxis and horse carriages from Qena, which can be reached by bus or train from Luxor
✋ Moderate

Palm trees grow in what was the Sacred Lake of the Temple of Hathor

Fascinating scenes of daily life in the rock tombs of Beni Hasan

EL-MINYA

The provincial town of Minya was a good base for visiting the surrounding antiquities and a pleasant place to be, until recently when Islamic militants made it less safe for foreigners. The town has a few dilapidated colonial buildings and an interesting Muslim and Coptic cemetery, Zawiyet el-Mayyetin, on the West Bank to which the dead were transported on *feluccas* until not long ago.

- 28C4
- 245km south of Cairo
- Governate Building, Corniche el-Nil, Luxor
- ☎ 086-320 150
- Lotus (£) on Sharia Port Said
- Trains from Cairo, Luxor

SOHAG

Sohag is a small town with a large Coptic community. Its main attractions are the nearby monasteries on the edge of the desert. Deir el-Abyad (White Monastery), founded in the 5th century by St Pjol and dedicated to St Shenuda, looks like a pharaonic temple. Once it was a thriving community of more than 2,000 monks, but only a few remain today. The smaller Deir el-Ahmar (Red Monastery) was founded by St Bishoi, a disciple of St Shenuda.

- 29D3
- 206km south of el-Minya, 472km south of Cairo
- Monasteries open daily 9–5 (free but donations welcome)
- Buses and trains from Cairo, Asyut, el-Minya and Luxor; monasteries reached by taxi only

TELL EL-AMARNA

The fascinating city founded by the rebellious pharaoh Akhenaten (1350–1334 BC) and his beautiful wife Nefertiti, was abandoned after 14 years, when the king died, and the priests from Karnak destroyed it as much as possible. They had left Thebes to establish Akhetaten, their new capital, dedicated to one god, the sun god Aton. The Royal Road passes the ruins of the Great Temple of Aton, the Royal Residence, the State Palace and the Sanctuary of Aten. On the other side of the landing post are the better preserved Temple of Nefertiti and the Northern Tombs of Amarna nobles with scenes representing the joyful life at the capital. The Southern Tombs, 14km away, are the finest, especially those of Mahu and Ay.

- 28C3
- 60km southwest of el-Minya
- Daily 7–4 in winter, 7–5 in summer
- Service taxis from Mallawi to el-Till, then blue tourist ferry or normal ferry across
- Tickets at the tourist office near the landing; prices vary. Bus tours are available as the site is large

TUNA EL-GEBEL

Only a small area of the vast necropolis is open to the public. Near the entrance is the Sacred Animal Necropolis for mummified baboons, ibises and other animals. Further south is the City of Dead, where the tomb of High Priest Petosiris (300 BC) has fine wall-paintings of agriculture, crafts and funerary processions.

- 28C3
- 50km south of el-Minya
- Daily 7–5
- Taxi only
- Moderate

75

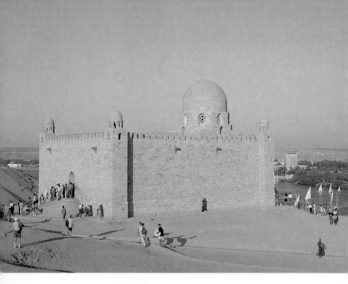

The Aga Khan found a solution for his health problems in Aswan, and fell in love with its wonderful climate and landscape

Aswan

Aswan, Egypt's southernmost town, feels more like Africa than the rest of Egypt. The people, mostly Nubians, are taller and darker than Upper Egyptians, their music and culture has more in common with the Sudan than with Cairo or Alexandria, and the smells are sweet and tropical. Two deserts, the Eastern Desert and the Sahara, close in on the Nile which here flows around a series of granite rocks and little islands. The First Cataract, which ancient Egyptians believed was the source of the Nile, once marked the end of the civilised world, as boats were unable to pass this natural barrier. Yebu on Elephantine Island was the Old Kingdom frontier, as well as an important cult centre. Today, as in ancient times, Aswan is renowned for its wonderful winter climate and beautiful setting.

What to See in Aswan

AGA KHAN MAUSOLEUM ⭐⭐

🚩 29D2
✉ West Bank of Nile
🕐 Closed to the public
🚤 *Felucca*, no public ferries
💷 Free

This small but dignified mausoleum was built for the third Aga Khan (1877–1957), the leader of the Ismailis, a Shi'ite Muslim sect. The Aga Khan, who was famous for his incredible wealth, fell in love with this spot and with Aswan. His widow spends winters in the villa below the mausoleum, and puts a fresh red rose on his tomb each day. The views over the Nile and Aswan are spectacular, especially at sunset.

The Nilometer was essential in fixing the level of taxes, which depended on the height of the Nile flood

MATHAF EL-ATHAAR ✪✪
(ASWAN ANTIQUITIES MUSEUM)

Housed in the villa of Sir William Willcocks, the British engineer who designed the old Aswan dam, the museum has a massive collection of objects found on Elephantine Island and a collection of artefacts salvaged from the flooded areas beyond the dam. Pottery, jewellery and statues from the Middle and New Kingdom are displayed on the ground floor, while there are some mummies in the basement and a superb gold-covered statue of Khnum. By the Nile is the Nilometer with Greek, Roman, pharaonic and Arabic numerals, a most important instrument as taxes were calculated according to the height of the Nile. Further south are the ruins of ancient Yebu. Beyond a gateway on which Alexander II is shown worshipping Khnum are the ruins of a 30th Dynasty Temple of Khnum. Although this is site is still being excavated, it is worth a visit for the spectacular views of Aswan and the Nile.

🕂 29D2
⊠ On tip of Elephantine Island
🕐 Daily 8:30–5 winter, 8:30–6 summer
🍴 Tea in the garden for a tip (£)
🚢 Ferry from the landing dock near EgyptAir office
♿ Moderate, includes visit to the Nilometer and ruins of Yebu

MATHAF EL-NUBA (NUBIAN MUSEUM) ✪✪✪

The Nubian Museum is a long-awaited tribute to the Nubian people whose lands were flooded after the construction of the Aswan Dam. In a beautiful modern building vaguely inspired by traditional Nubian architecture, the museum's well-displayed, well-labelled exhibits follow the history, art and culture of Nubia from prehistoric times (c4500 BC) to the present day. Among the highlights are the oldest skeleton found in the Toshka region, a superb statue of a 25th Dynasty Kushite priest of Amun and an interesting display explaining the development of irrigation along the Nile. A reconstructed Nubian house in the museum garden is not open at the time of writing.

🕂 29D2
⊠ Near the Basma Hotel
🕐 Daily 9–1, 5–10
♿ Few
♿ Moderate
❓ No photography

Felucca sailing around the Islands

Feluccas
Official prices for *feluccas* per person for every possible excursion including waiting time, are available from the tourist office:
✉ Northern end of the Corniche, next to Misr Travel
☎ 097-312 811

Distance
3km

Time
3–4 hours with stops

Start point
Docks by EgyptAir office on Corniche Road

End Point
Old Cataract Hotel

Rent a *felucca* from the docks near the EgyptAir office. Late afternoon is best, when the air is cooler and the light is softer, in time to catch the sunset in all its majesty. The *felucca* zigzags between Aswan Corniche and the Nubian villages on Elephantine Island.

On the west bank are the Tombs of the Nobles (open 7–5, till 6 in summer), which belonged to the princes and priests of Elephantine. The finest are the tombs of Sirenput I and II, with colourful scenes of daily life. Higher up is the tomb of a local *sheikh* (saint) known as the Qubbat el-Hawa (Dome of the Winds), with fantastic views of Aswan. Continue by *felucca* to the Botanical Gardens on Kitchener's Island (open 8–sunset), a lush, sweet-smelling island presented to the British general Lord Kitchener after his military successes in Sudan. Kitchener decided to have the island planted with exotic plants and trees from all over the world.

Sailing along the back of the Elephantine Island, you should catch a glimpse of village life, including little children who sing Nubian songs from their tiny boats hoping for some *baksheesh* (tips). On the west bank beyond Elephantine, the Aga Khan's Mausoleum (► 76) is also the stop for the 10th-century St Simeon's Monastery, destroyed in 1173 by Saladin. The steep climb (½ hour) through soft sand is rewarded by the spectacular, romantic setting of this roofless basilica. End by jumping off at the Old Cataract Hotel landing (► 103) for an apéritif on the terrace.

Feluccas *sailing in the late afternoon sun, seen from the Old Cataract Hotel's terrace*

EL-MESALA EL-NAKSA (UNFINISHED OBELISK) ★

This might have been the largest obelisk ever, 41m high and weighing almost 1,200 tonnes, but it was left unfinished in the quarry when a flaw in the granite was discovered. It was meant to be one of a pair, the other of which is the Lateran Obelisk, erected in the Temple of Tuthmosis III in Karnak but now in Rome.

✚ 29D2
✉ 2km south of Aswan on the road to Philae
🕐 Daily 7–5 (6 in summer)
▦ Moderate

PHILAE TEMPLES (▶ 25, TOP TEN)

SADD EL-ALI (HIGH DAM) ★★

The old Aswan dam, completed by the British in 1902, was soon found to be too small, but it wasn't until the 1960s that a new dam was built. President Nasser saw the High Dam as the key to making Egypt self-reliant, as controlling the Nile flood would provide electricity for the whole country. The High Dam is immense; 111m high, more than 3.8km long, 980m wide at the base, 40m at the top with a volume some 17 times that of the Pyramid of Khufu. Lake Nasser, the world's largest reservoir, at over 6,000sq km, has saved Egypt from famine and floods several times, and made it possible to irrigate vast stretches of desert. But it isn't all good news. As a result of the dam Nubians lost their land, ancient monuments were inundated by the lake (some were rescued by a UNESCO salvage operation), Nile silt no longer fertilises Egyptian fields and the ground-water level has risen, threatening monuments all along the Nile in Egypt.

✚ 29D2
✉ 7km south of the old Aswan dam
♿ Few
▦ Cheap
↔ Philae Temples (▶ 25)
❓ Photography of the dam is strictly forbidden, passport may be required

The enormous concrete structure of the High Dam, with the Russian-Egyptian Friendship Monument in the background

What to See in the Southern Nile Valley

DARAW ✪✪

The only reason people stop at Daraw is to visit its large camel market. Camels are brought across the desert along the Forty Days Road from Darfur and Kordofan in Sudan, to a place north of Abu Simbel. From there they are driven to Daraw and sometimes to Birqash near Cairo (➤ 45). The market is a fascinating place, especially in the early morning, when Sudanese traders in their traditional costumes prefer to do their business.

EDFU (TEMPLE OF HORUS) ✪✪✪

After Karnak (➤ 20–1), this is the largest temple in Egypt and also the best-preserved, having been buried in the sand and houses built over it until archaeologists uncovered it in the 1860s. Built in 237 BC by Ptolemy III and dedicated to the falcon god Horus, the temple stands on the site where Horus is believed to have fought his uncle Seth for control of the world. Much has been learned about this temple from building and foundation texts inscribed on the walls.

The entrance is now at the back of the complex, but the visit should start at the Grand Pylon to the south. On the outside Neos Dionysos (Ptolemy XIII) is shown slaughtering his enemies in front of Horus. The inner walls portray the annual Festival of the Beautiful Meeting, when Horus's statue was taken to Hathor's temple at Dandara (➤ 74). Two impressive statues of Horus front the Hypostyle Hall, which leads into the beautifully decorated Festival Hall and Hall of Offerings, the oldest part of the temple. The Sanctuary still contains the granite altar on which rested Horus's sacred boat, and the large granite shrine which the statue of the god once inhabited.

Sidebar (Daraw)

🚹 29D2
✉ 40km north of Aswan, 5km south of Kom Ombo
🕐 Every Tue 6:30AM–2PM, in winter also Sun AM, best before 10:30AM
🍴 Cafés (£)
🚌 Minibus or service taxi from Aswan to Kom Ombo, taxi to Daraw

Sidebar (Edfu)

🚹 29D2
✉ 115km south of Luxor, 105km north of Aswan
🕐 Daily 6–6 summer, 7–4 in winter
🍴 Café (£)
🚌 Service taxis from Aswan and Luxor; train and bus to Edfu from Aswan and Luxor, then taxis to the temple
📖 Moderate

Granite carving of the falcon god Horus at Edfu Temple

ESNA TEMPLE ✪✪

The temple of the ram-headed god Khnum was probably as large as Edfu after the reconstruction by Ptolemy VI (c180 BC), but most of it remains hidden under the village. Only the Hypostyle Hall, a 1st-century AD addition by the Roman emperor Claudius, has been excavated. Its 24 painted columns with capitals in the shape of different flowers and plants form an enclosed garden, while Roman emperors adorn the walls, making offerings to the Egyptian deities.

✚ 29D2
⊠ 54km south of Luxor, 155km north of Aswan
🕒 Daily 6–5:30 (till 6 in summer)
🚌 Buses from Luxor and Aswan stop a short walk away from the temple
✋ Moderate

KOM OMBO TEMPLE ✪✪

Most Egyptian temples were dedicated to a single deity, but Kom Ombo Temple, started by Ptolemy VI (c180 BC) and finished by Roman emperor Augustus (30 BC–AD 14), was dedicated to two: Horus the Elder and Sobek. The eastern side was devoted to the crocodile god Sobek, and the Chapel of Hathor near the entrance housed some mummified crocodiles. The other side of the temple was dedicated to Horus the Elder, known as the 'Good Doctor', and attracted sick pilgrims, who took part in complicated rituals here in the hope of a cure. The temple's dramatic location, on a bend in the river, was also its undoing – much of the pylon and the forecourt were swept away by the Nile, though a double entrance to the inner hypostyle hall survives with elegant floral columns. Behind the two sanctuaries there are seven chapels on whose outer walls is depicted an interesting display of medical instruments, clear evidence that ancient Egyptian surgeons performed highly sophisticated operations.

✚ 29D2
⊠ 170km south of Luxor, 45km north of Aswan
🕒 Daily 8–4
🍴 Kiosk with drinks (£)
🚌 Buses from Luxor and Aswan stop in town, 1.5km from the temple
✋ Moderate
↔ Daraw (➤ 80)

Detail of fine reliefs on the columns of the twin temples dedicated to Horus and Sobek at Kom Ombo

81

Below: *visitors are
dwarfed by the colossal
Osirid statues of
Ramses II in his temple
at Abu Simbel*

⊕ 29D1
✉ 280km south of Aswan
🕐 6AM–5PM or until the last
   plane leaves
🍴 Café (£)
🚌 Buses from Aswan
✈ From Cairo and Aswan;
   return tickets include
   transfers between the
   airport and site. If the
   outgoing plane is delayed
   there may be little time at
   the site
🏛 Moderate
❓ On 22 Feb and 22 Oct at
   dawn the sun rays touch
   the cult statues

Lake Nasser

**UNESCO relocated many Nubian temples
threatened by the building of the High Dam and the
creation of Lake Nasser. For many years, fishing
boats and the occasional ferry to Sudan had the
lake to themselves, but several cruise ships (➤ 103)
now operate between Aswan and Abu Simbel;
fishing trips are increasingly popular (➤ 114) and
several luxury hotels are planned.**

What to See at Lake Nasser

ABU SIMBEL ⊕⊕⊕

The two temples at Abu Simbel were built by Ramses II
and are the most spectacular Nubian monuments. The
façade of the Great Temple of Re-Harakhte is dominated
by four magnificent seated colossi of Ramses II, cut into
the cliff, flanked by other members of the royal family. The
Hypostyle Hall, lined with 10m-high Osirid statues of the
pharaoh, is decorated with superb reliefs of his famous
victories. The temples were hand-sawn out of the rock
face, cut into 1,050 blocks and reconstructed on an
artificial hill, the inside of which can be visited (entrance
beside the temple). Near by is the smaller Temple of
Hathor fronted by statues of Ramses II and Nefertari with
their children. The Hypostyle Hall, supported by Hathor-
headed columns, has reliefs of the queen watching her
husband at war. A cow statue of Hathor in the sanctuary is
decorated with reliefs of Nefertari and Ramses.

The elegant Roman Kiosk of Qertassi with four papyrus and two Hathor-headed columns

AMADA ✪

The oldest Egyptian temple in Nubia, Amada was built by Tuthmosis III and Amenophis II, dedicated to Amun-Re and Re-Harakhte. Reliefs in the inner right-hand chapel show the temple's foundation rituals. In the sand lie early drawings of animals (including elephants) carved on stone. Near by is the Rock Temple of el-Derr, built by Ramses II, with excellent colourful reliefs, and the rock-cut Tomb of Penne, viceroy of Nubia under Ramses VI, with traditional themes on the walls.

🞡 29D1
✉ 170km south of the High Dam
🕓 Daily 6–6
🚢 Cruise boat only
🎟 Free

KALABSHA ✪✪

Built during the great 18th Dynasty (1570–1293 BC) and rebuilt under the Ptolemies and Romans, Kalabsha was dedicated to the Nubian fertility god Marul (the Greeks called him Mandulis). Much of its later decorations have survived. The monuments were relocated here from other sites in Nubia when Lake Nasser was formed and the picturesque Roman Kiosk of Qertassi originally stood 10km away from Kalabsha. More interesting is Beit el Wali (the Governor's House), a small rock-hewn temple built by the Governor of Kush (Ethiopia) during the reign of Ramses II.

🞡 29D2
✉ Next to the High Dam
🕓 Daily 8–4
🚢 Taxi from Aswan. Temple itself can often only be reached by boat from the harbour
🎟 Cheap
🔁 High Dam (➤ 79)

QASR IBRIM ✪✪

Qasr (fortress) Ibrim remains where it was founded in c1000 BC, but what was formerly a mountain top dominating the Nile now only just manages to stay above Lake Nasser. Remains of a healing centre, dedicated to Isis, are visible, as are walls of a 10th-century Christian basilica. From the Ottoman invasion in 1517 until 1812 the castle was manned by Bosnian soldiers.

🞡 29D1
✉ 40km north of Abu Simbel
🕓 Daily 6–6
🚢 Cruise boat only
🎟 Free

WADI EL-SEBU'A ✪✪

Wadi el-Sebu'a (Valley of the Lions) was named after the 16 sphinxes which line the entrance. The highlights are the many statues and images of Ramses II, in whose reign this was built, and decorations from the time of early Christians, which make for some bizarre contrasts. The Temple of Dakka, reconstructed near by, was begun by Arkamani, a Meroite king contemporary with Ptolemy II (285–246 BC). Dedicated to Thoth, it is the only Egyptian temple facing north. Also here is the Roman temple of Maharraka, dedicated to Isis and Serapis, of which only the Hypostyle Hall survives.

🞡 29D1
✉ 135km south of the High Dam
🕓 Daily 6–6
🚢 Cruise boat only
🎟 Free

Suez Canal, Sinai & the Red Sea

The Suez Canal divides Africa from Asia, and Sinai from the rest of Egypt. The desert was too savage for Nile dwellers to settle, but that didn't stop them visiting the mountains on both sides of the divide to find gold (around the Wadi Hammamat), turquoise (at the 12th Dynasty [1990–1780 BC] mines around Serabit el-Khadem) and other minerals. Sinai was always an important transit route and many passed through, from Moses and the Hebrews to Christian hermits living around Wadi Feiran and St Catherine's Monastery, and Muslim pilgrims, thousands of years later, making their way to Mecca. Apart from their traces, the region's main attraction is the water and what lies beneath it. The days of pristine coastline are long gone, but there are still idyllic places in Sinai and along the Red Sea coast.

> *'At Old Kosseir the sea takes on fabulous colours, with no transition between them – from dark brown to limpid azure. The Red Sea looks more like the ocean than like the Mediterranean. So many shells!'*

GUSTAVE FLAUBERT
Carnets de Voyage
25 May 1850

———————●———————

The Gulf of Aqaba with the Saudi Arabian coastline in the far distance

One of many large cruise ships which drop anchor just off Port Said's busy harbourfront on the Suez Canal

Suez Canal

To reach the East from Europe before the 167km long canal was built meant either sailing around Africa or crossing the desert between Cairo and Suez. When the canal opened in 1869, Suez enjoyed a boom and the new towns of Port Said and Isma'iliya were created. But the Arab-Israeli conflict closed the canal, devastated the area (most of Suez was levelled and effectively abandoned between 1967 and 1973) and robbed the area of much of its wealth. Of the three, Port Said has recovered the best, helped by tax-free status. Since it was nationalised in 1956, the canal has been one of Egypt's largest sources of revenue.

What to See in the Suez Canal Area

BUR SA'ID (PORT SAID)

Port Said is no longer 'the wickedest town in the East' – no more dirty postcards or canalside brothels – but it still attracts sailors from around the world. The sights are few: the canal itself – the most captivating thing to see; the plinth at the mouth of the canal where a statue of De Lesseps, the engineer, stood until blown up in 1952; some 19th-century buildings, particularly along the waterfront. The **National Museum** has a small collection of antiquities and artefacts from the opening of the canal, including Khedive Ismail's carriage.

ISMA'ILIYA

The older, European-built quarter of the city retains its genteel air, typified by the Swiss-style house of Ferdinand de Lesseps, who dreamed and schemed the canal into existence. The dusty museum, built like a Ptolemaic temple, has a small collection of Graeco-Roman and phaoronic artefacts. The city's other main attraction is its beaches, where you can watch freighters pass by.

29D5
225km from Cairo, 85km north of Isma'iliya
Sharia Filastine ☎ 066-235 289
Cafés/restaurants (£–££)
Buses from Cairo, Suez, Ismai'liya, Hurghada

National Museum
Sat–Thu 9–4, Fri 9–11, 2–4

29D5
120km east of Cairo, 85km from Port Said
Cafés/restaurants (£–££)
Buses from Cairo, Hurghada, Port Said

Sinai

Sinai, sitting between Africa and Asia, is a place of rugged landscapes and natural beauty. While most of its coastline is being developed into beach resorts and diving centres, the interior remains a desolate mountain desert with some important Christian holy places and Bedouin communities fighting hard to maintain traditions.

What to See in Sinai

The coast may have been taken over by international tourist resorts but the interior of Sinai is till Bedouin territory

DAHAB ✪

Dahab (Arabic for gold), with its superb beaches and coral reefs, is still considered one of Sinai's best dive sites. The town divides into the Bedouin settlement of el-Asla, the up-market hotels of el-Mashraba and the camps of el-Masbat where backpackers and old hippies hang out. It may be the most relaxed town in Egypt, but beware of bathing topless which is illegal, and of drugs, still widely available although the police are getting tougher. Bedouins organise camel treks into the magnificent desert interior, but Dahab's main sights are undoubtedly under the water, particularly at the Blue Hole and the Canyon (➤ 89).

🚹 29E4
✉ 100km northeast of Sharm el-Sheikh, 570km from Cairo
🍴 Several restaurants in all price categories
🚌 Regular buses from Sharm el-Sheikh, Taba, Nuweiba, Cairo
♿ Few

DEIR SANT KATARIN (ST CATHERINE'S MONASTERY) (➤ 19, TOP TEN)

NUWEIBA ✪

Nuweiba was a thriving resort during the Israeli occupation but now there is little to see or do. The town is divided between the dull port area and the tourist village on a pretty sandy beach. Day-trippers come from Sharm el-Sheikh to swim with a wild dolphin who befriended a local Bedouin. Other Bedouins organise camel treks to the spectacular Coloured Canyon.

🚹 29E4
✉ 72km north of Dahab
🍴 Restaurants (£–£££)
🚌 Regular buses from Cairo, Sharm el-Sheikh, Dahab, Suez and Taba
⛴ At least 1 daily ferry to Aqaba (4hrs) in Jordan

29E3
⊠ 30km from Sharm el-Sheikh
🕐 Sunrise–sunset; camping permits are issued by the visitors' centre
🍴 Restaurant (£–££)
🚕 Taxis or organised tours
💷 Cheap
❓ Passport and visa needed for UN checkpoints

29E3
⊠ 470km from Cairo
ℹ️ Naama Bay ☎ 062-660 600
🍴 Cafés/restaurants (£–£££)
🚌 Buses from Cairo, Dahab, Nuweiba, Suez and Taba
🚂 from Cairo and Luxor
⛴ Ferry from Hurghada several times a week ☎ 062-544 702

29E4
⊠ 390km from Cairo
🍴 Taba Hilton (£££)
🚌 Daily buses from Cairo and Sharm el-Sheikh
✈️ Flights from Cairo to Ras an-Naqb airport (39km)

RAS MUHAMMAD   ✪✪✪

Ras Muhammad, Sinai's southernmost tip, was declared Egypt's first national park in 1988. The 12 per cent of the park that can be visited tends to be overwhelmed by day trippers from Sharm el-Sheikh during high season. Its sandstone mountains, *wadis* (dry gullies) and soft sand dunes are inhabited by foxes, gazelles, ibexes and migratory birds. The stunning coral reefs are a famous haunt for manta rays, sharks and hawksbill turtles, while the magnificent mangroves are breeding grounds for migratory and resident birds.

SHARM EL-SHEIKH   ✪✪

Sharm el-Sheikh was developed, mostly for military purposes, by the Israelis when they occupied Sinai between 1967 and 1982. Over the past few years Sharm has become Sinai's main resort, with many more hotels being built. The Naama Bay area has the highest concentration of hotels and best facilities for watersports, as well as good snorkelling off the beautiful reef. The only sight is Ras Kennedy, a rock resembling the former US president John F Kennedy's face.

TABA   ✪

Taba, a small beach resort on the border with Israel, was returned to Egypt in 1989 after ten years of negotiation. The coastline is beautiful with bays, coves, lagoons and an island. On Geziret el-Faraun (Pharaoh's Island) stands the 12th-century fortress of Salah el-Din, the most important Islamic monument on the Sinai peninsula.

Sun, sea, sand – and a touch of the Orient on the beach at Sharm el-Sheikh

Top Red Sea Diving & Snorkelling Sites

Sinai

- **Blue Hole** (a few kilometres north of Dahab). Pleasant, easy diving and snorkelling on the outer reef of the Blue Hole lagoon, with mainly hard corals and a large variety of reef fish.
- **The Canyon** (on the way to the Blue Hole, Dahab). A long, narrow and very beautiful canyon, with plenty to see even for inexperienced divers.
- **The Islands** (near Laguna Hotel, Dahab). Spectacular labyrinth of coral peaks, bowls and corridors, teeming with fish and the occasional turtle.
- **End of the Road Reef** (extreme end of Nabq coastal road, north of Sharm el-Sheikh). Submerged island with some of the best corals in Egypt. Abundant fish life.
- **Shark Observatory** (Ras Muhammad). A vertical wall of soft and hard coral which attracts barracuda, grey and blacktip sharks and Napoleon fish.
- **Ras Ghozlani** (Ras Muhammad). Nicest spot on the southern coast to observe the abundant small reef species and well-preserved corals.

A diver meets a scary looking Crown of Thorns

Red Sea

- **Carless (Careless) Reef** (5km north of Giftun Island). Famous for its semi-tame moray eels, but untamed sharks and jacks can often be spotted.
- **Green Hole** (59km north of Quseir). Magnificent coral growth, dolphins and blue-eagle rays as well as the usual reef species.
- **Beit Goha** (20km north of Quseir). Exceptional, very shallow, coral garden, still in great condition, with sturgeon fish, grouper, trumpet fish and many others.
- **Sirena Beach Home Reef** (in front of Mövenpick Hotel, Quseir). Just off the jetty is a reef with a huge variety of both corals and fish, including giant schools of tuna, Napoleon and lion fish.

The Red Sea coast as it used to look, but now rarely does, as a line of tourist resorts is being planned from Suez down to the Sudanese border

Red Sea Coast

Ancient Egyptians looked for gold, copper and precious stones in the Red Sea mountains, while early Coptic saints Anthony and Paul took refuge here from Roman persecutors and in due course founded the world's first monasteries. Today much of the 1,600km of coast from Suez to the border of Sudan, with its beautiful sandy coves and magnificent coral reefs, is being developed into beach resorts and its fragile habitat is increasingly coming under threat.

What to See on the Red Sea Coast

EL-GHARDAKA (HURGHADA) ⭐

Hurghada has developed fast, some say too fast, from a tiny fishing village into one of Egypt's most popular destinations. The town and its tourist bazaar is of little interest, but large beach resorts offering a wide variety of watersports make up for that. The water is warm for much of the year and there is a cooling breeze in the hot summers. For those not into diving or snorkelling there is the Sindbad Submarine (▶ 110), a small Red Sea Aquarium (▶ 110) and the museum of Marine Biology, 5km north of town.

🞣 29D3
✉ 529km southeast of Cairo
🛈 Sharia Bank Mist
☎ 065-546 513
🍴 Restaurants (£–£££)
🚌 Daily buses from Cairo, Luxor, Aswan and Suez
✈ Flights from Cairo, Luxor, Sharm el-Sheikh and St Catherine

EL-GOUNA ⭐

A new up-market resort with a few five-star hotels, a residential area with holiday homes for wealthy Cairenes, an 18-hole golf course and several shallow lagoons. El-Gouna has its own airport, an aquarium and a small museum with good replicas of ancient Egyptian treasures.

🞣 29D3
✉ 30km north of Hurghada
🍴 Restaurants (£–£££)
🚌 Taxis from Hurghada
✈ Flights from Cairo and Luxor ☎ 02-301 5632

EL-QUSEYR (QUSEIR) ⭐

Until the 10th century the largest port on the Red Sea, the sleepy town of Quseir, overlooked by a 16th-century fort, offers a welcome alternative to the crowds of Hurghada. There is wonderful snorkelling off the beaches and this is a good base from which to explore the deep south.

🞣 29E3
✉ 80km south of Hurghada
🍴 Hotel restaurants (££–£££)
🚌 No public transport

Where To...

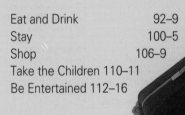

Above: *a camel with a traditional colourful bridle*
Right: *Egyptians usually laugh in the face of adversity*

Cairo & Environs

Price categories
Prices are for a meal for two without drinks or service.

£ = less than 60LE
££ = 60–140LE
£££ = more than140LE

Absolut (££)
This trendy hotspot for young wealthy Cairenes serves good snacks and plays loud music amid a modern Oriental decor.

✉ 10 Midan Amman, Mohandiseen ☎ 02-336 5583
🕐 Dinner only

Abu Shakra (£)
Known as the 'King of Kebab' this is one of the best places in Cairo to eat a simple and plain kebab.

✉ 69 Sharia Qasr el-Aini, Garden City ☎ 02-364 8811
🕐 All day

Alfi Bey (£–££)
Simple Egyptian cooking is served with a smile at this atmospheric old-fashioned restaurant. Start with *mezze* (appetisers), followed by pigeons stuffed with *firik* (crushed wheat) or a lamb kebab, and finish with rice pudding or *mahallabiya* (dessert made of flour). No alcohol.

✉ 3 Sharia El-Alfi, Downtown
☎ 02-577 1888/577 4999
🕐 1AM–1PM

Americana Fish Market (££)
A spacious boat moored on the Nile where you can choose your fresh fish or seafood from the display, then tell the chef how you would like it cooked. Salads are equally well prepared and be sure to try a dessert from the trolley.

✉ 26 Sharia el-Nil, Giza ☎
02-570 9693 🕐 12:30PM–2:30AM

Andrea (£–££)
Delightful garden restaurant, with an indoor room for the evenings and cold days. Excellent roasted chicken and grills with Oriental salads and freshly baked *baladi* bread. Children's play area in the garden.

✉ 59–60 Marioutiya Canal, El-Ahram, Giza ☎ 02-383 1133
🕐 Noon–1AM

Arabesque (££)
Cosy restaurant, popular with Egyptian movie stars and French expatriots, tucked away behind an art gallery. Although the French dishes are excellent, the thing to try here is *meloukhiya* with chicken or rabbit, pigeons with Oriental rice and one of the best *Umm Ali's* (milky bread pudding with coconut, raisins and cream) in town.

✉ 6 Sharia Qasr el-Nil, Downtown ☎ 02-574 7898
🕐 Lunch, dinner

l'Aubergine (££)
Simple bistro cuisine (meat and vegetarian) and jazz are on offer at this very laid-back restaurant, popular with foreigners who live in the area. The Curnonsky bar upstairs is good for a beer and to eavesdrop on foreign correspondents, who often hang out here.

✉ 5 Sharia Sayed el-Bakri, Zamalek ☎ 02-340 6550
🕐 8AM–2AM

Egyptian Pancake House (£)
Delicious sweet and savoury *fateers*, a cross between a pancake and a pizza.

✉ Between Sharia el-Azhar and Midan el-Husayn, Khan el-Khalili 🕐 All day

Estoril (££)
Well-prepared Levantine cuisine and friendly, old-fashioned service in this

long-established restaurant popular with actors, journalists and artists.

✉ 12 Sharia Talaat Harb, Downtown ☎ 02-574 3102
🕐 Lunch, dinner

Felfella Garden (£)

The original of a growing chain which offers a good introduction to traditional Egyptian cuisine in kitsch and exotic surroundings. A large selection of salads, *fuul* (fava bean) dishes and grilled meats at very reasonable prices.

✉ 15 Sharia Hoda Shaarawi, Downtown ☎ 02-392 2833
🕐 7AM–midnight

El-Fishawi (£)

Arguably the oldest teahouse in Cairo, claiming never to have closed since 1773. A great place to sip tea, smoke a waterpipe and watch the world go by. No alcohol.

✉ Just off Midan el-Husayn, Khan el-Khalili 🕐 All day

Flying Fish (££–£££)

Known as Omar Sharif's favourite restaurant, with excellent fresh fish, seafood and very good lobster.

✉ 166 Sharia el-Nil, Agouza ☎ 02-349 3234 🕐 Noon–1AM

Jounieh (£££)

Excellent, smart Lebanese restaurant and bar, with good views of the Nile from the outdoor terrace and live Arabic entertainment. Try the tender meat grills or a succulent *kibbeh* (pounded meat and wheat), followed by refreshing watermelon with ice-cream.

✉ Corniche el-Nil, opposite the World Trade Centre, Boulaq ☎ 02-575 9709 🕐 Noon–3AM

Moghul Room (£££)

A good place to recover from a hectic day, this elegant and beautifully decorated restaurant serves authentic Indian food, with soothing live Indian music every night.

✉ Mena House Oberoi Hotel, Sharia el-Ahram, near the Giza Pyramids ☎ 02-383 3222/3444
🕐 Lunch, dinner

Naguib Mahfouz Coffee Shop (£) & Khan el-Khalili Restaurant (££)

The only up-market place to eat in the bazaar (as well as the only decent toilets) with traditional Egyptian drinks, waterpipes and sweets in the coffee shop and *mezze* (appetisers) and traditional dishes in the restaurant. Mainly for tourists, but a cosy and quiet place to retire from the busy streets.

✉ 5 el-Badestan alley, Khan el-Khalili ☎ 02-590 3788
🕐 10AM–2AM

Al-Omdah (£)

Serves the best *kushari* (rice, macaroni, lentils, chickpeas and fried onions, topped with a spicy tomato sauce) in town. The branch around the corner serves a 'salad only' menu, with fresh fruit juices.

✉ 6 Sharia el-Gazayer, off Gamaat el-Dowal el-Arabeya (near the Atlas Hotel), Mohandiseen ☎ 02-345 2387
🕐 Noon–2AM

Papillon (££)

A well-established and popular Lebanese restaurant in the Mohandiseen area offering an extensive menu of interesting dishes from the Middle East.

✉ Sharoa 26 July ☎ 02-347 1672 🕐 Dinner only

Peking (££)

Fresh, tasty Chinese food in a romantic decor, which gets even more atmospheric when the house speciality dessert of Irish coffee is served, accompanied by taped bird music.

✉ 14 Sharia Saraya el-Ezbekiya, behind Cinema Diana, Downtown ☎ 02-591 2381
🕐 Lunch, dinner

A Waterpipe and Mint Tea

On a hot balmy Cairene evening, after dinner in one of the city's many restaurants, head for the cafés around Midan el-Husayn. The area is very lively until after midnight, and packed during religious festivals (► 116). The many cafés, including El-Fishawi and El-Sukkariya, serve fresh fruit juices, herbal teas, coffee and a digestive mint tea. Egyptians love to watch the world go by whilst smoking a *sheesha* (waterpipe) with *tumbac* (tobacco), *maassal* (tobacco with molasses) or *tuffah* (tobacco sweetened with apple), and you shouldn't leave the country without trying it.

Juice bars

One of the pleasures of Cairo are the colourful tiled juice bars with pyramids of oranges, strawberries and guavas announcing their trade. Juices are cheap and usually freshly squeezed on the spot. Try whatever is in season: sweet sugarcane, orange, carrot, delicious mango, pomegranate, guava or strawberry, or the local version of a milkshake, milk with bananas.

Prestige (£–££)

Stop for a quick meal in the pizzeria or enjoy the romantic atmosphere in the restaurant with its tablecloths and soft candlelight.

✉ 43 Sharia Gezoret al-Arab ☎ 02-347 0383 🕓 Lunch, dinner

Rigoletto (£)

Home-made American-style ice-creams, excellent ice gateaux and a rather good cheesecake. Popular with young Zamalekawis.

✉ 3 Sharia Taha Hussein, Zamalek ☎ 02-340 8684 🕓 All day

Samakmak (££)

No menu, just select your fish from the catch of the day, have it fried or grilled, and it will be served with rice, bread and salads. After a delicious meal, have a waterpipe while overlooking Cairo traffic.

✉ 92 Sharia Ahmed Orabi, Mohandiseen ☎ 02-347 8232 🕓 10AM–5AM

Simmonds Coffee Shop (£)

Good place for a breakfast pastry at the bar washed down with fresh fruit juice and for coffee all day.

✉ 112 Sharia 26 July, Zamalek 🕓 All day

El-Sukkariya (£)

Old café in a quiet back street of the bazaar, where local traders come for their waterpipe and tea. Later at night it is slightly more family-orientated and often the atmosphere is livened up even more with a storyteller, relating his age-old stories accompanied by *oud* (lute) music.

✉ Behind the Naguib Mahfouz café, Khan el-Khalili 🕓 All day, best at night

Sushiyama (£££)

One of the city's best Japanese restaurants, with a large menu of authentic *sushi, sashimi, tempura* and grills.

✉ World Trade Centre, 1191 Corniche el-Nil, Boulaq ☎ 02-580 4066/578 5161 🕓 Lunch, dinner and take-away

Taj Mahal (££)

Delectable Indian food served in a minimalist stylish decor. Good vegetarian dishes as well as spicy meat curries. Try a *gulab jamun* (dumplings soaked in syrup) to round off your meal.

✉ 15 Midan Ibn Afaan, entrance on Sharia el-Hegaz, Mohandiseen ☎ 02-348 4881 🕓 Lunch, dinner

Les Trèfles (£££)

French/Mediterranean cuisine is served in the elegant dining room or on a small terrace overlooking Zamalek and the Nile. You can expect to find rich Cairenes, dressed up, out to see and be seen. The food is excellent and, for Cairo, extremely expensive.

✉ Corniche el-Nil, opposite the World Trade Centre, Boulaq ☎ 02-579 6511 🕓 Lunch, dinner

Zinc (££)

Cool bar-restaurant decorated with plenty of metal and silver and gold colours, serving *tapas* and pastas to a trendy young crowd of Egyptians and foreigners.

✉ 157, 26th of July Street, Zamalek, in a side street behind Maison Thomas ☎ 02-340 9640 🕓 Dinner only

Faiyum

Café Gabal el-Zinah (£–££)

Pleasant café-restaurant with splendid views over the lake and mainly fish on the menu. There is a children's playground and a boat landing with colourful rowing boats.

✉ Birket Qarun 🕓 All day

Alexandria & the Oases

Alexandria

Cap d'Or (£)
Great art nouveau bar with some original decoration, French pop music and excellent fish dishes – including fried calamari and squid stew – to accompany cold Stella beers.

✉ 4 Sharia Adib, off Sharia Saad Zaghloul ☎ 03-483 5177
🕐 Lunch, dinner

Fish Market (££–£££)
An up-market fish restaurant with excellent fish, good service and sweeping views of the bay and harbour.

✉ El-Kashafa el-Bahariya Club, 26 Corniche el-Nil ☎ 03-480 5114 🕐 Lunch, dinner

Hassan Bleik (£)
Cheap, atmospheric Lebanese restaurant with old waiters and wonderful food such as chicken with almonds and Lebanese stuffed pigeon.

✉ Opposite 12 Sharia Saad Zaghloul ☎ 03-484 0880
🕐 Lunch only

Samakmak (££)
Opposite the boat-builders yard near the fish market, this unpretentious restaurant is everything you would expect a fish restaurant to be. There is both indoor and outdoor seating, and the very fresh fish you choose from the counter is grilled or fried as you wish.

✉ 42 Qasr Ras et-Tin, el-Bahry ☎ 03-480 9523 🕐 Lunch, dinner

Spitfire Bar (£)
Popular 1970s bar, playing good old rock 'n' roll and filled to the brim with memorabilia and pictures from loyal customers, including American sailors, many of whom like to drop in when at anchor.

✉ 7 Sharia el-Bursa el-Qadima ☎ 03-480 6503
🕐 Noon–2AM (or later)

Zephyrion (££)
Delightful Greek-run family fish restaurant outside Alexandria, with a pastel-painted terrace overlooking the Mediterranean. Very popular with Alexandrian families at weekends.

✉ 41 Sharia Khaled Ibn Walid, Abu Qir ☎ 03-560 1319
🕐 Lunch, dinner

The Oases

Abdu's (£)
Apart from the restaurant at Adrere Amellal Hotel (► 102), this is the best place in town for Egyptian food as well as couscous and pizzas.

✉ Opposite Yusuf Hotel, Siwa
🕐 Breakfast, lunch, dinner

Handy's (£)
Meeting place of everyone travelling through town, serving simple, good food.

✉ Dakhla 🕐 Breakfast, lunch, dinner

Popular Restaurant (also known as Bayyoumi's) (£)
The only place to eat in Bahariya, serving edible meat and vegetable stews, bread, omelettes and soup.

✉ At the main intersection of el-Bawiti, Bahariya 🕐 Breakfast, lunch, dinner

Restaurant of El Badawiyya Hotel (£–££)
One of the best restaurants in the oases. Well-prepared, freshly cooked Egyptian food served in a courtyard.

✉ Farafra 🕐 All day

Alexandria's Patisseries
One of the best places to look for 'Old Alexandria' is in its many old-fashioned patisseries. Try Athineos at 21 Midan Saad Zaghloul; Trianon at Midan Zaghloul; the pleasant garden at Baudrot, 23 Sharia Saad Zaghloul; the elegant sugary decor at Venous, 12 Sharia el-Hurriya or the most classic of all, Pastroudis at 39 Sharia el-Hurriya, which has a wonderful terrace to while time away.

Nile Valley & Nubia

Karkadeh
Many hotels in Upper Egypt offer a glass of sweet *karkadeh* as a welcome drink. This delicious dark red infusion of dried hibiscus flowers can be drunk hot in winter, but is usually served ice-cold. It is also used in cocktails mixed with gin or vodka. Dried hibiscus flowers are cheap and can be bought anywhere in Egypt, but are particularly good in the *souk* in Aswan.

Aswan
Aswan Moon (£)
Popular Nile-side restaurant with a mock castle entrance and a terrace on a floating pontoon. The food is fine, especially if you stick to the Egyptian *mezze* (appetisers) and stews, and the fresh fruit juices are a treat, but it's the ambience most people come for. This is the meeting place for young Aswanis in search of beer, *felucca* captains singing Nubian songs and tourists enjoying views of the river or trying to organise a boat trip.
✉ **Corniche el-Nil** ☎ **097-326 108** 🕐 **Lunch, dinner**

Aswan Panorama (£)
Waterfront café-restaurant serving simple Egyptian *mezze* (appetisers) and other dishes, as well as drinks and fresh juices. For those who want something quieter than the lively atmosphere at the Aswan Moon.
✉ **Corniche el-Nil, beside the Aswan Moon** 🕐 **All day**

Darna (££)
Pleasant restaurant designed as an Egyptian house serving a buffet with traditional dishes. One of the few places in Aswan with a good selection.
✉ **New Cataract Hotel, Sharia Abtal el-Tahrir** ☎ **097-316 002** 🕐 **Dinner only**

Al-Misri Tour Restaurant (£)
With a men-only room in the front and family room at the back, this rather quaint but very clean place serves some of the best *koftas* and kebabs in town, so it can be hard to get a seat.
✉ **Sharia el-Matar, off Sharia**

el-Suq; ask for directions, as everyone knows it 🕐 **All day**

1902 Restaurant (£££)
Rather average international cuisine is served in this elegant, turn-of-the-century Moorish dining hall. Nubian dancers and musicians add spice to the experience.
✉ **Old Cataract Hotel, Sharia Abtal el-Tahrir** ☎ **097-316 000** 🕐 **Dinner only**

Old Cataract Terrace (££)
This splendid hotel terrace for tea or at sunset has become one of the sights. The view is spectacular and Earl Grey tea with cakes and sandwiches is a treat, but beware that there is a steep minimum charge for non-residents from 4PM to sunset.
✉ **Old Cataract Hotel, Sharia Abtal el-Tahrir** ☎ **097-316 000** 🕐 **All day**

Luxor
Caféteria Mohamed (£)
Simple restaurant in a West Bank house where you can sample real Egyptian food. Small menu, but give Mohamed some warning and he will prepare a delicious *meloukhiya* (vegetable soup), stuffed pigeon or grilled kebabs, all served with cold beer.
✉ **Next to the Pharaoh's Hotel, near the ticket office on the West Bank** 🕐 **Lunch, dinner**

Class (££–£££)
Rather impersonal up-market restaurant serving adequate international food and a few Oriental classics. Very cold air conditioning!
✉ **Sharia Khaled Ibn Walid, next to the Isis Hotel** ☎ **095-386 327** 🕐 **Lunch, dinner**

...ing's Head Pub (£–££)

...British pub with all the ...immings: darts, pub food, ...lliards, football on TV and ...ts of British tourists happy ... have found a home away ...om home.

⬛ **Sharia Khaled Ibn el-Walid** 🕐 **Evenings**

...ushari Sayyida Nefisa (£)

...ot great on decor and ...tmosphere, but definitely ...e best *kushari* (a mixture of ...acaroni, rice, fried onions ...nd lentils) in town.

⬛ **Sharia Mustapha Kamel, ...ear the *souk*** 🕐 **All day**

...a Mamma (££)

...n Italian restaurant set in a ...easant garden with a pond ...ll of wading birds and ...elicans. The fresh pastas ...nd meat dishes are good, ...nd the live entertainment in ...e evening makes for a ...ongenial atmosphere.

⬛ **Sheraton Hotel, Sharia ...halid Ibn Walid** 🕐 **095-374 ...4** 🕐 **Lunch, dinner**

...laratonga Café- ...estaurant (£)

...his lovely shady terrace is a ...ood place to stop for lunch ..., after a long day of ...ghtseeing, to see the late ...fternoon sun shine orange ...n the magnificent temple. ...ou can either stop for a ...rink or try the simple but ...ell-prepared Egyptian ...shes.

⬛ **Opposite Madinet Habu ...emple** 🕐 **All day**

...larsam Hotel Restaurant ...)

...he food is cheap and tasty, ...ainly Egyptian fare, and ...ere is a good chance that ...ou'll run into some of the ...rchaeologists excavating in

the neigbourhood. Best in spring and autumn.

⬛ **Opposite the Valley of the Nobles, West Bank** 🕐 **095-372 165** 🕐 **Lunch, dinner**

Mövenpick Restaurants (££–£££)

Good fresh food such as salads, pizzas and kebabs are served on the beautiful terrace by day, with views over the Nile and the green bank on the other side. At night there is an indoor buffet or à la carte menu. The Swiss ice-creams are a speciality.

⬛ **Crocodile Island, 5km from Luxor Centre** 🕐 **095-374 855** 🕐 **Lunch, dinner**

Royal Bar (£)

Old-fashioned colonial bar, perfect for an early evening aperitif or beer.

⬛ **Old Winter Palace, Corniche el-Nil** 🕐 **095-380 422** 🕐 **Afternoons and evenings**

Tutankhamun (£)

One of many restaurants near the ferry landing, but Tutankhamun is by far the best. The chef and owner used to cook in one of Luxor's five star hotels. Chicken with rosemary, served with sweet Oriental rice, is a speciality.

⬛ **Near the public ferry landing on the West Bank** 🕐 **Lunch, dinner**

El-Minya
Lotus (£–££)

The Lotus hotel's rooftop restaurant is one of the best places to get a decent meal in Minya, and has good views over the Nile and the town.

⬛ **1 Sharia Port Said** 🕐 **086-324 541** 🕐 **All day**

Food Markets

The best place to buy fresh produce for a picnic or a long-distance *felucca* trip is the market. In Luxor, beyond the tourist *souk* on Sharia el-Birka, there are a few fruit and vegetable stalls as well as groceries. On Tuesdays there is also a fruit and vegetable market on Sharia Television, Luxor. A more atmospheric market is held in the village of New Gurnah on the West Bank, every Tuesday morning. In Aswan head for Sharia el-Souk, near the station.

Suez Canal, Sinai & the Red Sea

Bedouin Lunch

Several travel agents in Sinai and on the Red Sea offer camel or horse safaris for one day or longer, which include lunch in a tent, which often belongs to a Bedouin family. The food is traditional Bedouin fare of roast mutton or lamb, and three servings of tea – to accept more is considered rude. Check with Fantasea Dive Club, Dahab ☎ & fax 062-640 043; Sanafir, Sharm el-Sheikh ☎ 065-600 197.

Suez Zone
El-Borg (£–££)

A simple restaurant serving some of the best fish and seafood in Egypt. Seafood soup contains just about all the seafood you can find here, while the sole fillets and sea bass are served perfectly grilled with lemon. Just heavenly. No alcohol, but you can bring your own.

☒ **Near the beach in Port Said; just ask for directions as everybody knows it** ⊕ **Lunch, dinner**

George's (££)

Cairenes come for the day to sample George's famously fresh seafood and fish.

☒ **Sharia Sultan Hussein, Isma'iliya** ☎ **064-288 363** ⊕ **Lunch, dinner**

Nora's Floating Restaurant (££)

Lunch and dinner cruises with good Egyptian food, and of course, an excellent view of the Suez Canal. Departure times do vary but officially noon and 8PM.

☒ **Sharia Filastine, opposite the National Museum, Port Said** ⊕ **Lunch, dinner**

Sinai

Sharm el-Sheikh
Bus Stop (££)

Trendiest place in town, with a façade and interior shaped like a bus. Sounds tacky but it is actually quite fun, and the place turns into a discothèque later at night. The rooftop bar in the Sanafir is the other place to be seen, especially earlier in the evening.

☒ **Sanafir Hotel, Naama Bay** ☎ **062-600 197** ⊕ **7PM onwards**

Café Bedouin (£)

Situated on terraces built against the cliffs of Naama Bay, the café is very atmospheric, with little lanterns in locally made pottery, caged monkeys and even a Chinese pagoda. Sweeping views over the bay and a good place to catch the breeze on a hot evening.

☒ **Sharm Panorama, Naama Bay** ⊕ **7PM onwards**

Café el-Fishawi (£)

An Egyptian café around a fountain in the bazaar, where you can smoke a waterpipe with touffah (sweet apple tobacco) and drink mint tea.

☒ **At the heart of Sharm Mall, opposite the Sanafir Hotel, Naama Bay** ⊕ **10AM–midnight**

Dananeer (££)

One of the more characterful places to eat on this strip. Fresh seafood and fish dishes as well as traditional Egyptian specialities such as meloukhiya (vegetable soup with rabbit, and pigeons stuffed with wheat.

☒ **Main Street, Naama Bay** ☎ **062-600 321** ⊕ **Lunch, dinner**

Hard Rock Café (£–££)

Casual atmosphere and the usual memorabilia which belonged to rock stars such as Madonna, Elton John and Elvis Presley.

☒ **Naama Bay** ☎ **062-602 6** ⊕ **12:30PM–2AM (3AM at weekends)**

Fish Restaurant (£££)

Quiet outdoor fish restaurant, decorated with fishing nets and other fishing paraphernalia, serving excellent French fish and

eafood dishes. Service can
e erratic.
🔳 Near diving centre, Hilton
ayrouz, Naama Bay ☎ 062-
0 136 🕓 Dinner only

irates Bar (££)
opular venue for an evening
rink, in a romantic garden
ith bridges over little
onds. Happy hour 6–7PM.
🔳 Hilton Fayrouz, Naama Bay
☎ 062-660 136 🕓 Evening

amTam (£–££)
arge menu with simple but
xcellent Egyptian food
erved in a canteen-like
door restaurant or on the
ore pleasant terrace.
🔳 Ghazala Hotel, Naama Bay
☎ 062-600 150/9 🕓 Lunch,
nner

Which Way (£–££)
errace restaurant
verlooking the hotel pool
here good-value, well-
epared *mezze* (appetisers)
e served with cool beers.
void the pizzas.
🔳 Hotel Kahramana, Naama
ay ☎ 062-601 071/2/3 🕓
nch, dinner

ed Sea

l-Ghardaka
Hurghada)
elfella (£–££)
ranch of the popular
airene chain (► 93) serving
ood and reasonably priced
gyptian fare.
🔳 Sharia Sheraton ☎ 065-
2 410 🕓 Lunch, dinner

alian Restaurant (££–£££)
elicious and inventive
alian dishes, home-made
astas and tender *involtini*
tuffed veal rolls), served on
romantic garden terrace.
🔳 Intercontinental Hurghada

Hotel ☎ 065-443 911 🕓
Dinner

Portofino (££)
Italian fish and seafood
specialities as well as fresh
home-made pasta are served
in this pleasant Italian
restaurant.
🖂 General Hospital Street, al-
Dahar ☎ 065-546 250
🕓 Lunch, dinner

El-Sakia (££)
Private beach with spacious
outdoor restaurant in a
garden. Popular with ex-
patriates and better-off
Egyptians, this is one of the
best places to sample local
fish and seafood. Choose
your fish from the pond.
🖂 On the beach in Sekala ☎
065-442 497 🕓 Lunch, dinner

El-Gouna
Kiki's Café (££)
Popular restaurant with two
open-air terraces offering
great views over the town
and lagoons. The food is
excellent with fresh home-
made pastas and salads.
🖂 Above the museum in Kafr
el-Gouna 🕓 Dinner

**Sayyadeen Fish Restaurant
(££)**
Airy and spacious fish
restaurant on the beach with
a large terrace, serving
excellent fish and seafood.
🖂 Mövenpick Hotel, on the
beach ☎ 065-545 160
🕓 Lunch, dinner

Zeytouna Beach Bar (£–££)
Funky bar, beautifully
decorated, with its own
private beach.
🖂 On the small island south of
the Miramar Hotel, reached by
water taxi in front of the Gouna
Museum 🕓 All day

Fuul, Fuul, Fuul
One of Egypt's most
popular dishes is
undoubtedly *fuul,* or fava
beans, stewed in water for
12 hours. Cheap and
wholesome, often eaten
for breakfast, it is a
favourite at all levels of
Egyptian society. Everyone
has their own trick to
customise this earthy
brown stew – try it with
lemon and cumin, green
pepper, egg, oil or
tomatoes. There is a
superstition that eating too
much *fuul* is bad for the
brain and the diet of *fuul* is
often cited as the cause of
the nation's woes, from
the lethargy of bureaucrats
to the crazy driving in
Cairo's streets.

Cairo & Environs

Hotel prices
Prices are for a double room with bathroom

£ = less than US$30
££ = US$30–100
£££ = over US$100

Atlas Zamalek (££)
Modern hotel in a lively area with many shops and restaurants near by. The hotel discothèque is popular with expatriots. It has a swimming pool on the roof and all business facilities.
✉ **20 Sharia el-Duwal el-Arabiya, Mohandiseen** ☎ **02-346 5782, fax 02-347 6958**

Cairo Marriott (£££)
Khedive Ismail's sumptuous palace on the Nile, built for the celebrations marking the opening of the Suez Canal in 1869, has been turned into the central area of the Marriott Hotel. Rooms in the two modern towers lack atmosphere but have splendid views over the Nile and city. The bedroom of the French empress Eugenie is now Eugenie's Lounge, an elegant cocktail bar, and there is a swimming pool in the khedival gardens. The garden Promenade is a popular terrace café for a drink or lunch.
✉ **Sharia Saray el-Gezira, Zamalek** ☎ **02-340 8888, fax 02-340 6667**

Cosmopolitan (££)
Right in the centre but in a surprisingly quiet back street, this magnificent art nouveau building has spacious and comfortable rooms.
✉ **1 Sharia Ibn Tahlab, Downtown** ☎ **02-392 3845, fax 02-393 3531**

Garden City House (£)
A dusty but charming 1930s pension-style hotel which is a favourite with scholars and archaeologists. Half-board is compulsory but the simple food is quite good and

conversations at the table can be enlightening.
✉ **23 Sharia Kamal el-Din Saleh, behind the Semiramis Hotel, Garden City** ☎ **02-354 4969**

Golden Tulip Flamenco (££)
Modern hotel in a residential area at the back of the island of Zamalek, close to shops and restaurants, with clear cosy rooms. Some rooms overlook the Nile and even have views of the Giza pyramids on a clear day. Good Spanish restaurant.
✉ **2 Sharia el-Gezira el-Wusta, Zamalek** ☎ **02-340 0815, fax 02-340 0819**

Horus House (££)
Very quiet hotel in residential area, often booked in advance by regular visitors to Cairo who like its friendly, homely atmosphere. The restaurant offers a good-value lunch, and has amongst its regulars some older couples who live on the island.
✉ **21 Sharia Ismail Muhamad, Zamalek** ☎ **02-340 3977**

Ismailiya House (£)
A backpackers' haven with clean, cheerful rooms and dormitories, MTV and an excellent laundry service, overlooking the square (noisy) or Downtown Cairo. Book well in advance.
✉ **7th floor, 1 Midan Tahrir, Downtown** ☎ **02-356 3122**

Lotus (£)
Very central, friendly budget hotel with spotless rooms, some of which have bathrooms. Book in advance.
✉ **Malev Airline Arcade, 7th floor, 12 Sharia Talaat Harb,**

...wntown ☎ 02-575 0627, fax
...575 4270

...ayfair (£)
...nall quiet hotel in a tree-
...ed street with spotless
...oms, some with a balcony
...erlooking the street.
...anquil terrace for having an
...ternoon drink.
☒ 9 Sharia Aziz Osman,
...malek ☎ 02-340 7315

...ena House Oberoi (£££)
...ooms in the more
...pensive 19th-century wing
...this former khedival
...nting lodge are stylish and
...autifully decorated, and
...me have wonderful views
...er the nearby pyramids.
...ost rooms, however, are in
...e modern garden annexe,
...hich is less characterful,
...hough it shares similar
...ews. The Moghul Room
... 93) is considered the
...st Indian restaurant in
...wn, while the Rubayyat
...ghtclub features some of
...e best belly dancers in the
...ea.
☒ Sharia el-Ahram ☎ 02-
...3 3222, fax 02-383 7777

...le Hilton (£££)
...he of the first modern
...ernational hotels in Egypt
...th an authentic ancient
...atue in its lobby. The
...mfortable rooms either
...erlook the Nile or
...owntown Cairo, and the
...rs and restaurants are
...pular meeting places for
...ealthy Cairenes and
...patriates.
☒ Corniche el-Nil/Tahrir
...uare ☎ 02-578 0444, fax 02-
...3 0475

...nsion Roma (£)
... old-style 1940s hotel
...th clean rooms, polished
...ooden floors and nice old
...rniture. Very popular with
...avellers, so it is advisable
... book ahead.
☒ 169 Sharia Muhamad Farid
☎ 02-391 1088

President (££)
Small, comfortable, mid-
range hotel in a quiet
residential street with all
business facilities and some
rooms with views of the
Nile. Good value.
☒ 22 Sharia Taha Hussein,
Zamalek ☎ 02-340 0652, fax
02-361 0874

**Saqqara Country Club and
Hotel (££)**
Well-run tranquil hotel in the
green Saqqara countryside,
with stables and riding
facilities. Temporary day
membership to the country
club from the reception.
☒ Saqqara Road to Abu el-
Nomros ☎ 02-384 6115, fax 02-
385 0577

Victoria (££)
Near Ramses station, this
noisy, characterful 1940s
hotel has spacious, spotless
rooms with mahogany
furniture and air-conditioning.
Delightful little café-terrace
in the garden.
☒ 66 Sharia Gumhuriya, Midan
Ramses, Downtown ☎ 02- 589
2290, fax 02-591 3008

Windsor (£–££)
Well-run budget hotel,
considered Downtown's
best, in a Moorish-style
building with clean spacious
rooms, arched windows and
high ceilings. Delightful
colonial-style bar on the first
floor, totally musty and old-
fashioned. Book in advance.
☒ 19 Sharia el-Alfi, Downtown
☎ 02-591 5277, fax 02-592 1621

Faiyum
**New Panorama Shakshuk
(££)**
Best resort hotel in the area.
Modern air-conditioned
rooms have balconies
overlooking the lake. Sports
facilities include duck
shooting, fishing, wind
surfing and waterskiing.
☒ Birket Qarun ☎ 084-701
314, fax 084-701 757

A Hotel Like No Other
The El-Hussein Hotel at
Midan el-Husayn, Islamic
Cairo ☎ 02-918 664/918
089 is rather run down but
uniquely situated in the
heart of the Islamic city,
with balconies overlooking
the busy square outside
the mosque of Husayn.
Don't hope to sleep during
festival times. In spite of
the loud noise from
muezzin calling for prayers
five times a day and
wedding parties
celebrating all night long,
the atmosphere is great.
Try the roof terrace for a
drink and to see the sun
set over the old city's
domes, minarets and TV
antennae.

Alexandria & Oases

Ecology in the Oases

Tours of the Western Desert oases are becoming increasingly popular, but the fragile desert environment is already showing the strain. Basic environmentally friendly practices such as taking all rubbish away with you and burning all toilet paper seem obvious but are not always observed. Many antiquities here are under threat as some guides show more concern for profit and self-promotion, helping tourists to take away antiquities, inscribe their names on the rocks or spray water on prehistoric rock paintings to get better pictures. For recommended desert guides ➤ 114.

Alexandria

Acropole (£)

Greek-run top floor pension. The clean, characterful rooms are filled with old wooden furniture that has seen better days, but some enjoy the same views as the much more expensive neighbouring Cecil Hotel.

✉ 27 Rue Chambre de Commerce ☎ 03-480 5980

Helnan Palestine (£££)

A favourite amongst old Alexandrian families, this quiet hotel with its private beach and bay is slightly overrated these days, but all rooms have balconies with views of the Mediterranean.

✉ Muntazah Palace garden ☎ 03-547 3500, fax 03-547 3378

Paradise Inn Metropole (££)

This period hotel has charming rooms with high ceilings and lots of atmosphere. Excellent and friendly service. Serious competition for the neighbouring Cecil as the best central hotel. Book in advance.

✉ 52 Sharia Saad Zaghloul ☎ 03-482 1465, fax 03-482 2040

Sofitel Alexandria Cecil Hotel (££–£££)

Lawrence Durrell immortalised the Cecil in his *Alexandria Quartet* so the hotel still attracts romantics, but although the views over the bay are magnificent, the glamour has long gone. Erratic service.

✉ 16 Midan Saad Zaghloul ☎ 03-483 4768, fax 03-483 6401

Oases

Adrere Amellal (££)

Wonderful eco-lodge with simple but comfortable rooms lit by oil lamps, its own farm and natural spring pool. Food is fresh from the farm and simply delicious.

✉ Just outside Siwa ☎ No phone number at the time of writing

El-Beshmo Lodge (£)

The most pleasant hotel in town, on the edge of a palm grove opposite the Roman hot spring of the same name. Simple but spotless and comfortable rooms with private or shared bathroom

✉ 10-minute walk from main street, el-Bawiti, Bahariya ☎ & fax 018-802 177

El Badawiyya Safari and Hotel (£)

One of the best hotels in the Oases, tastefully designed in mudbrick. The clean, domed rooms have private or shared bathrooms. Owned by local Bedouins, but run by a Swiss woman. Book in advance.

✉ Main street, Farafra ☎ 02-345 8524

Pioneers Hotel (£££)

The first four-star hotel in the Oases, the Pioneers has comfortable air-conditioned rooms and satellite TV. Same owners as the equally salmon-pink painted, three-star Mut Talata in Dakhla (☎ 092-821 530).

✉ Kharga ☎ 092-927 982, fax 092-927 983

Siwa Safari Paradise (££)

Wonderful setting in a beautiful palm grove, though the architecture is more prosaic. The rooms are slightly tacky, but clean and comfortable.

✉ Siwa town ☎ 046-460 2289/90, fax 092-460 2286

Nile Valley & Lake Nasser

swan

noun (££–£££)

is small hotel, now run by
ub Med, on a island
erlooking the Old Cataract
d the desert on the other
nk of the Nile, is a great
ace to relax. It has a
imming pool, simple but
mfortable rooms and the
od, though variable, is
nerally good.

⊠ Amoun island (free ferry
from the EgyptAir office) ☎
-313 800, fax 097-317 190

eopatra (£–££)

maculate rooms with
ephone and private
throom and a small pool
the roof terrace.

⊠ Sharia Saad Zaghloul, near
souk ☎ 097-324 001, fax
-314 002

fitel Old Cataract (£££)

e Old Cataract has
come one of the sights in
wan and tea on the
rrace at sunset is a must.
e grand hotel, which
atured in Agatha Christie's
eath on the Nile, was
ened in 1899 and is
obably Egypt's most
nous hotel. Filled to the
m with nostalgia, its
autiful rooms command
onderful views over the
e and Elephantine Island.

⊠ Sharia Abtal el-Tahrir ☎
-316 002, fax 097-316 011

xor

non el-Gazira (£)

at rare thing, a well-kept,
mily-run hotel set amidst
lds, with very clean rooms
ith and without private
throoms), a roof terrace
th marvellous views of the
est Bank and a lovely
rden where breakfast is
rved. Book in advance.

⊠ Geziret el-Bairat, West
Bank (near the ferry landing, left
at the Mobil petrol station)
☎ 095-310 912

Marsam Hotel (known as Sheikh Ali Hotel) (£)

Run by the son of Sheikh Ali
who helped excavate the
tomb of Seti I and whose
family were renowned tomb
robbers, this pleasant
mudbrick hotel is popular
with regular visitors to Luxor.
Accommodation is clean and
basic, the nights are magical
and quiet. Great atmosphere
and friendly service.

⊠ Opposite the Valley of the
Nobles, West Bank ☎ 095-372
403

Mina Palace (£)

Old-fashioned building with
clean air-conditioned rooms,
with TV and Nile views, or a
view over Luxor Temple.
Excellent value.

⊠ Corniche el-Nil, near Luxor
Temple ☎ 095-372 074

Mövenpick Jolie Ville Luxor (£££)

The best hotel in Luxor with
quiet, if dated, rooms in
bungalows set in a
wonderful well-kept garden.
Good food, famous ice-
cream, excellent service,
great swimming pool and a
little zoo for children.

⊠ Crocodile Island, 6km south
of Luxor, near the new bridge
☎ 095-374 855, fax 095-374 936

Sofitel Old Winter Palace (£££)

Another grand colonial hotel
on the Nile with large high-
ceilinged rooms and great
views of the river and the
Theban Hills.

⊠ Sharia Corniche el-Nil ☎
095-380 422, fax 095-374 087

Cruising on Lake Nasser

The easiest way to see the
Nubian monuments
(➤ 82–3) is to cruise on
Lake Nasser. Boats take
three or four days to sail
from Aswan to Abu
Simbel, stopping at
temples along the way.
Recommended boats
include the MS Eugenie,
with wonderful pre-
revolution decor, excellent
food, health club and
swimming pool, or the
smaller Kasr Ibrim, owned
by the same company
Belle Epoque Travel at 17
Sharia Tunis, New Maadi,
Cairo ☎ 02-352 8754, fax
02-353 6114).

Suez Zone, Sinai & the Red Sea

Endless Building
Hurghada was a little fishing village until a few years ago but it is now the centre of a solid strip of hotel resorts stretching for many miles north and south along the coast. New resorts are being built further south at Safaga, Quseir and Marsa Alam, forcing serious divers ever further south. The entire Red Sea coast in Egypt, from Suez to the Sudanese border, has been divided up, and apart from some national parks, most has been handed over to developers. So if you are looking for untouched reefs and pristine coastline, come soon.

Suez Zone

Helnan Port Said Hotel (£££)
Best hotel in Port Said with all facilities, rooms overlooking the Mediterranean and an excellent private beach.
✉ El-Corniche, Port Said ☎ 066-320 890, fax 066-323 762

Mercure Forsan Island (££)
By far the best and most peaceful hotel in Isma'iliya with comfortable rooms, private beach with watersports and good views over Crocodile Lake.
✉ Forsan Island, northeast of Isma'iliya ☎ 064-765 322, fax 064-338 043

Nora's Tourist Village (££)
Large tourist village with rooms overlooking the beach, friendly service and good food.
✉ El-Corniche, Port Said ☎ 066-329 834, fax 066-329 841

Sinai

Basata (£)
Very popular camp with huts and bungalows on the beach. Those who stay here, from Egypt, Israel and Europe, enjoy the totally relaxed atmosphere. House rules include no drugs, alcohol or loud music. Meals are healthy, natural and communal, there is a desalination plant, and preservation of the coral reefs is high on the agenda.
✉ Ras el-Burg on the Taba–Nuweiba road, 42km south of Taba ☎ 062-500 481, fax 062-500 481

Hilton Fayrouz Village (£££)
One of the first resorts in Naama Bay, with bungalows set in a beautiful garden w bougainvillea. Large choice of restaurants and bars, ar a private beach.
✉ Naama Bay, Sharm el-Sheikh ☎ 062-600 136, fax 0 601 040

Moon Beach (££)
Good holiday resort with simple, comfortable room away from the crowds, wi excellent windsurfing facilities, suitable for beginners.
✉ At Km98 sign on the road from Ras Sudr to el-Tor, 290k from Sharm el-Sheikh, 190km from Cairo ☎ 062-291 5023, 062-336 5103

Nesima Dive Club and Hotel (££)
Beautiful new hotel with l of domes and arches, sim but comfortable rooms an great relaxed atmosphere Also has an excellent divi club.
✉ Dahab ☎ 062-640 320, 062-640 321

Pigeon House (£)
One of the cheapest place to stay in Naama Bay with clean modern rooms, acrc the road from the public beach.
✉ Naama Bay, Sharm el-Sheikh ☎ 062-600 996, fax 600 995

Safety Land Camp
As Naama Bay has gone more up-market, this is on of the few places affordab to backpackers. Simple thatched huts and tents v several beds.
✉ Sharm el-Moya ☎ & f 062-660 395

Sanafir (££)
One of the more characte

hotels in the bay with comfortable Moorish-style rooms set around a pleasant large courtyard and swimming pool. Not on the beach but guests can use the beach of the Aquanaute Diving Club.

✉ Naama Bay, Sharm el-Sheikh ☎ 062-600 197, fax 062-600 196

Victoria Resort Mövenpick Sharm el-Sheikh (£££)

Huge family resort, popular with European package tourists, with bungalows set in a quiet garden, large swimming pool, and all watersports facilities. Daily children's entertainment club.

✉ Naama Bay, Sharm el-Sheikh ☎ 062-600 100, fax 062-600 111

Red Sea

Dawar el-Omda (££)

Beautiful hotel built in a modern interpretation of traditional Nile-valley architecture, tastefully decorated with antiques and modern furniture designed by young Cairene designers.

✉ El-Gouna ☎ 065-545 060, fax 065-545 561

El-Giftun Village (££)

One of the oldest holiday resorts with all facilities for windsurfers and divers. Comfortable bungalows are set on the beach. Several bars and restaurants and all watersports are available.

✉ Hurghada ☎ 065-442 665, fax 065-442 666

El-Khan (£–££)

Smaller hotel with charming rooms set around a peaceful courtyard, overlooking the lagoon. Popular with young Cairenes.

✉ El-Gouna ☎ & fax 065-549 701

Mangrove Bay Resort (££)

Charming resort, still very quiet, with excellent diving and snorkelling facilities.

✉ 29km south of Quseir ☎ 065-348 6748, fax 065-360 5458

Mashrabia Village (££)

Excellent hotel, designed in a pseudo-Moorish style, with several swimming pools and very good watersports on offer.

✉ South of the port, Sharia Sheraton, Hurghada ☎ 065-443 330, fax 065-443 904

Miramar Sheraton (£££)

Architect Michael Graves designed the Miramar on several islands around a lagoon, facing the sea. There is a touch of Disney to the accommodation buildings, though the interior design owes much to the Mediterranean. All watersports facilities are available as well as a golf course.

✉ El-Gouna ☎ 065-545 606, fax 065-545 608

Mövenpick Quseir (£££)

Peaceful hotel, beautifully designed, with spartan, Nubian-style domed rooms and excellent service. Perfect retreat to get away from it all, with some of Egypt's best snorkelling and diving off the hotel's private beach.

✉ El-Quadim Bay, Quseir ☎ 065-432 100, fax 065-432 128

Red Sea Diving Safari (£–££)

Owner Helmy, a lawyer, environmentalist and enthusiastic diver, has set up a small eco-friendly resort with spotlessly clean and comfortable tents, huts and chalets. Mainly aimed at divers, but non-divers looking for peace and quiet will enjoy this place as well.

✉ At Marsa Shaqara, 20km north of Marsa Alam ☎ 065-339 9942, fax 065-349 4219

Wrecked Ships

There is more to see in the Red Sea than coral gardens and shoals of fish. Several interesting shipwrecks make for good diving expeditions, especially around the dangerous Straits of Gubal, at the mouth of the Gulf of Suez between Hurghada and Sharm el-Sheikh. Diving clubs organise special trips to see these and other wrecks.

Bookshops

Egyptian Music
Cairo is still the centre of Arab culture, so it is a good place to be initiated into the region's music. Kiosks in downtown Cairo sell pirated tapes of inferior quality, so watch what you buy. One of the best places to buy good-quality CDs and tapes of the classics such as Umm Kalthum, Farid el-Atrash and Abdel Wahaab is at Sono Cairo on Sikket Ali Labib Gabr, opposite Radio Cinema, off Sharia Qasr el-Nil, Downtown. For funky new wave Arab music check out Abdullah in the alley behind l'Americaine on Sharia Tallat Harb. Nubian and Sudanese music can be bought in kiosks in Aswan or from a few shops along the flyover just off Midan Opera in Cairo.

Cairo
Anglo-Egyptian Bookshop
Good selection of books about Egypt and the Arabic world, especially history, politics and culture, as well as classic paperbacks.
✉ **165 Sharia Mohammed Farid, Downtown** ☎ **02-391 4337**

AUC Bookshop
Probably the most extensive range of books on Egypt and the Middle East, many published by the American University Press, as well as the latest English literature.
✉ **American University, 113 Sharia Kasr el-Aini , in Hill House on the main Campus, Downtown** ☎ **02-357 5377 and** ✉ **16 Sharia Mohammed Ibn Thakeb, Zamalek** ☎ **02-339 7045**

Lehnert and Landrock
Wonderful German, English and French bookshop with a large section on ancient and modern Egypt, Islam and the Arab world. They also sell copies of interesting old photographs of Cairo and Upper Egypt, new and old postcards and other Egyptian paraphernalia.
✉ **44 Shari Sherif, Downtown** ☎ **02-392 7606/393 5324**

Livres de France
Very good selection of mainly French books on Egypt, well-produced art books and French literature, as well as a few English books. Good children's section.
✉ **36 Sharia Kasr el-Nil, Downtown** ☎ **02-393 5512**

L'Orientaliste
Great but expensive bookshop packed full of dusty first editions and more valuable second-hand books and old maps about Egypt, Orientalism or the Middle East in general. You can expect to pay international prices.
✉ **15 Sharia Kasr el-Nil, Downtown** ☎ **02-575 3418**

Zamalek Bookstore
A good bookshop with mainly books on Egypt in several European languages, foreign newspapers and magazines and good-quality stationery.
✉ **19 Sharia Shagaret el-Dor, Zamalek** ☎ **02-341 5184**

Alexandria
International Language Bookshop
One of the better bookshops in Alexandria, with a good selection of travel books on Egypt and guides in several languages.
✉ **18 Sharia Abdel Hamid El-Dib, Tharwat** ☎ **03-586 6388**

Luxor
el-Aboudi
Books on Egypt in German, English, French, Spanish and even Japanese, as well as a large selection of postcards and books for children on Egypt and the pharaohs.
✉ **Tourist Bazaar, Corniche el-Nil, next to the Winter Palace Hotel** ☎ **095-373 390**

Gaddis
A great shop with books in many languages covering both modern and ancient Egypt, as well as postcards, Egyptian stationery in papyrus and some good-quality souvenirs.
✉ **Tourist Bazaar, Corniche el-Nil, next to the Winter Palace Hotel** ☎ **095-372 142**

Clothes & Fabrics

Cairo

Atlas Silks

This tiny shop continues a long tradition of making exquisite moiré fabrics in a wide variety of colours as well as tailoring clothes in both Oriental and Western style. They also make shoes in the same fabric.

✉ el-Badestan alley, Khan el-Khalili ☎ 02-590 6139/591 8833

Haberdashery

Several shops around el-Fishawi café (► 93) sell the basic belly dance attire, but the 'king' of belly dance costume shops is Haberdashery, who export to belly dancers all over the world. The showroom is filled with glittering, intricately designed dresses as well as belts, head ornaments, brass cymbals and jewellery. Belly dancers try out the outfits in front of a mirror while performing moves to the loud accompaniment of the latest belly dance tapes.

✉ A dark stairway, signed 'Everything a Belly Dancer Needs', on Sharia Gawhar el-Qayed, Khan el-Khalili near el-Fishawi café

El-Khiyamiya (Tentmakers Bazaar)

Well-preserved roofed market, where the traditional crafts of appliqué work and tentmaking are still practised in several tiny workshops. You can order one of the magnificent tents in a patchwork of Islamic designs, or just a cushion cover or wallhanging for a child's room with folkloric scenes from Egypt.

✉ Just outside Bab Zuwayla, Islamic Cairo

Ouf

A wide range of cheap cotton clothing, funky flowery fabrics, bed sheets, tablecloths and Bedouin-style embroidered dresses is on sale here.

✉ First alley to the left off the Spice Bazaar, which is the alley running along the Madrasa of Sultan Barsbay, off el-Muzz lidin Allah

Safari

Locally made cotton casual wear, perfect for T-shirts or travelling clothes. Reasonable prices and good quality. Watch out for the children's T-shirts with maps of Egypt or a camel caravan.

✉ 10 Sharia Lutfallah, beside the Marriott Hotel, Zamalek ☎ 02-340 1909 and at the World Trade Centre ground floor ☎ 02-774 261 and inside the Nile Hilton, Downtown ☎ 02-579 0845

Tanis

Wonderful cotton and linen fabrics, mostly for furnishings, carrying modern interpretations of pharaonic motives or simply camels and palm trees. Look out for the curtain gauze, with Arabic calligraphy or Ottoman star and crescents printed white on white.

✉ World Trade Centre, 1st floor ☎ 02-777 972

Luxor

Winter Akhmim Gallery

Akhmim in Upper Egypt has been known for centuries for its fine handwoven fabrics, and this shop specialises in colourful tablecloths and bedspreads.

✉ Old Winter Palace Hotel, Corniche el-Nil, East Bank ☎ 095-380 422

World Trade Centre

The WTC , 1191 Corniche el-Nil, is Egypt's largest and most up-market shopping mall. If you have little time and are looking for clothes, both locally made and imported, then this is the place to go to. It is also where wealthy Cairenes like to hang out, so there are several restaurants, bars and discothèques.

Aswan *Souk*

Running parallel to the Coniche is Aswan's *souk*, which is more exotic than most in Egypt. It can be very hot during the day, but shops are open late, so take an evening stroll. The market is famous for *karkadeh* (dried hibiscus flowers), from which a infusion is brewed, and for spices and peanuts from Sudan. Brightly coloured Nubian baskets and hand-woven silk scarves are well-made here. Also keep an eye out for magic charms, fetishes and dried crocodiles.

Handicrafts

Art Galleries

Cairo has seen the opening of many art galleries in recent years, many of them Downtown, with a lot more work coming from young Egyptian artists as well as foreigners living in Egypt. Check out *Egypt Today* and *Insight* magazines as well as the daily *Egyptian Gazette* for the latest shows. Places to keep an eye on include Atelier du Caire, 2 Sharia Karim el-Dawla; Cairo-Berlin Art Gallery, 17 Sharia Youssef el-Guindy; Mashrabia, 8 Sharia Champollion and Townhouse Gallery of Contemporary Art, Sharia Hussein Pasha, off Sharia Mahmoud Bassiouni, all Downtown.

Visiting Luxor's West Bank

The best way to visit the West Bank is to take your time and, if possible, to spread it over two or three days. If time is short, rent a taxi for the day to take you around. Otherwise, by renting a bike near the ferry on the West Bank you will also be able to enjoy the countryside. Tickets can only be bought from the central ticket office near the Temple of Madinet Habu (► 72), so you must decide there what you want to see. Check which tombs are open as some may be temporarily closed to avoid damage from over-visiting.

Cairo and Environs

Al-Ain Gallery

This gallery exhibits Azza Fahmy's wonderful contemporary silver jewellery, decorated with Arabic inscriptions, as well as stylish traditional metal work, including lanterns and lighting by Randa Fahmy.

✉ 73 Sharia el-Hussayn, Dokki ☎ 02-349 3940

Beit Sherif

When Zaki Sherif returned a few years ago from New York to his native Egypt, he started collecting antiques and royal memorabilia as well as designing his own lighting and furniture. His designs, inspired by the past but with a quirky modern edge to them, can be found in Cairo's trendy bars and restaurants, as well as in hotels in Gouna.

✉ 18b Sharia Marashli (also in Kafr el-Gouna, Red Sea) ☎ 02-341 5250

Dr Ragab's Papyrus Institute

This institute was founded by former ambassador Dr Hassan Ragab, who revived the making of papyrus to help preserve and promote this ancient Egyptian art. The museum displays the different stages of the making of papyrus and has a sales room on the first floor where you can buy top-quality papyri at top prices.

✉ Corniche el-Nil close to the Cairo Sheraton, Giza ☎ 02-348 8676

Fagnoon

Amazing furniture made in Egyptian woods such as mango and sycamore or in metal and glass, by Egyptian artists with a taste for the exotic. If you are into the unusual then this is worth checking out.

✉ Fagnoon Art School, Saqqara Road, Sabil Om Hashim, Giza and at World Trade Centre, 1191 Corniche el-Nil, Boulaq

Khan Misr Tulun

A wonderful treasure trove filled with some of the best handicrafts from all over Egypt. A world away from most of what is on sale in Khan el-Khalili.

✉ Facing the main entrance o the Ibn Tulun Mosque, Sayyida Zaynab ☎ 02-365 2227 🕔 Closed Sat, Sun

Marketing Link

Marketing Link is a non-profit-making organisation trying to sell and promote Egyptian crafts, from kilims and embroidered clothes from Northern Sinai to hand-woven tablecloths from Akhmim, recycled paper from Cairo and colourful baskets from Aswan. These high-quality products bear no relation to what is on sale in tatty tourist bazaars. Definitely worth checking out.

✉ 27 Sharia Yahia Ibrahim, 1st floor, apt 8, Zamalek ☎ 02-341 5123

Nagada

Beautiful hand-woven cotton fabrics and tablecloths in natural colours, fabric lanterns and fabulous pottery made in Faiyum, all tastefully displayed in this flat.

✉ 8 Sharia Dar El-Shefa, 3rd floor, Garden City ☎ 02-594-3249/341 4500 🕔 Mon–Sat 10–2, afternoons by appointment

Nomad Gallery

A floor of an elegant Zamalek residence filled with original Bedouin jewellery and rugs, as well as traditional designs in silver, and textiles and many types of baskets, mostly handmade in Egypt.

✉ **14 Saraya el-Gezira, 1st floor, Zamalek (and smaller branch in garden of the Cairo Marriott Hotel, Zamalek)** ☎ **02-341 1917**

Sadek el-Mansoury

This is a great little shop with all kinds of old and new beads from the more precious amber to the cheap but fun copies of ancient Egyptian *shabtis* (small statues of gods) and scarabs. They also sell good copies of statues of ancient Egyptian gods, especially the huge gold-leafed ibises.

✉ **Alley opposite Naguib Mahfouz Café, Khan el-Khalili** ☎ **02-591 1325**

Senouhi

Worth looking for, this hard-to-find shop (ring the doorbell if the door is closed) is an Aladdin's cave filled with Wissa Wasef carpets, old jewellery, embroidered clothes from Siwa, old postcards and books and felt puppets for children. Look out for the embroidered trousers and waistcoats for both adults and children, and the fifties-style postcards.

✉ **54 Shari Abdel Khaled Sarwat, 5th floor, apt 51, near Midan Opera** ☎ **02-391 0955**

Sheba Gallery

An interesting gallery with a selection of traditional and contemporary silver jewellery, textiles, pottery and small gifts.

✉ **6 Sharia Sri Lanka, Zamalek** ☎ **02-340 9192**

A Touch of Glass

Modern Egyptian-made glass, often inspired by Ottoman glassware is on sale here. Look out for simple glass plates and beautiful multicoloured tumblers, decorated with stars and crescent.

✉ **4–8 Shari el-Sjeikh el-Marsafi, off Shari Gezira, Zamalek** ☎ **02-341 2392**

Luxor

Egypt Crafts

Connected to Marketing Link in Cairo (► 108) this showroom sells crafts from all over Egypt at fixed prices, and offers a fair share to the producers. Akhmim weavings, Nubian baskets and interesting local pottery.

✉ **Next to the Marsam Hotel, el-Gournah, West Bank** ☎ **095-372 403**

El-Gournah

Objects and clothes, designed with a touch of humour by a couple of French artists – buttons with eye of Horus or embroidered holders for mineral water bottles – are made from local materials and by local artisans. The shop also functions as a gallery.

✉ **Opposite the Tomb of Ramoze, Valley of the Nobles, West Bank**

Sharm el-Sheikh

Aladin

Tiny shop with small antiques, Bedouin textiles and a good selection of glass beads, scarabs and hand-carved sea urchin bones.

✉ **In the El-Diar Hotel, Naama Bay** ☎ **062-600 826**

Glass Blowing

Glass making was probably introduced in Egypt by Asian artisans during the reign of Tuthmosis III, around 1500 BC, and happily it is still being practised. The rustic Muski glass is still produced by blowing recycled glass into new shapes: green and brown glass comes from beer and wine bottles; for clear glass manganese is added to the mixture, while copper filings are added to make turquoise glass. The most famous glass maker is el-Daour in Cairo, which can be reached by foot from Bab el-Futuh (► 34). Stand outside the gate and walk across the small square, turn right up Sharia el-Hussariya. Take the first left onto Sharia El-Beiraqdar and follow the narrow twisting alley to the end, which runs into the factory (open Sun–Thu 7:30AM–sunset).

Bedouins

Sinai's dwindling community of Bedouins are increasingly being settled into dull concrete villages without any employment prospects, and only a few remain semi-nomadic. The coastline is being developed, with most profits going to Cairene entrepreneurs and foreign companies, not to the local community. The largest Bedouin settlement is in el-Arish in Northern Sinai, which has a Bedouin market on Thursdays.

Children's Attractions

Children's Lunch

Don't worry about taking children to restaurants. Egyptians adore children, especially little ones, and you will usually find one or more waiters cooing over your child or offering to entertain them. Children will particularly like some of the more unusual restaurants such as Felfella (➤ 93) in Downtown Cairo, with its displays of live animals, and Andrea in Giza (➤ 92) which offers a playground, occasional donkey rides and the possibility of watching bread being baked.

Felucca Sailing

One of the most relaxing things to do on a hot afternoon is to hire a *felucca* (➤ 78), take a picnic and watch life along the river and its banks. The best place to do it is Aswan, but it is fun everywhere, even in Cairo. Boatmen usually let children steer for a while.

Glass-bottomed Boats

Most resorts, both in Sinai and along the Red Sea, offer daily trips in glass-bottomed boats, which allow visitors who are not so keen on diving or snorkelling the chance to explore the wonders of the Red Sea.

Red Sea Aquarium

Small aquarium with species from the Red Sea in well-marked tanks.

✉ 6 Sharia el-Corniche, next to Three Corners, Hurghada ⏰ Daily 8–5

Sindbad Submarine

A fun and exciting way to explore the wonders of the Red Sea by submarine, which goes down some 20m.

✉ Hurghada ☎ 065-444 688 (for reservations) ⏰ Daily from 9AM

Horse Riding

Children will love riding through the desert near the pyramids. Rather than getting hassled by persistent horse- and camel-drivers around the pyramids, use the authorised stables near the *son et lumière* by the Sphinx, who have calmer horses more used to children.

AA stables ☎ 02-385 0531
MG stables ☎ 02-385 3832

Arabian Horse Stable

The stable provides camels, donkeys and horses for both adults and children to explore the countryside or the desert on the West Bank.

✉ Behind the Mobil petrol station, near the ferry landing on the West Bank ☎ 095-310 024 ⏰ Daily

Museums

Mathaf el-Masri (Egyptian Museum)

This vast museum is wonderful for both children and adults alike. Children will be particularly fascinated by Tutankhamun's treasure (including bows, daggers and chariots), the mummy room and models representing ancient Egyptian life on the first floor (➤ 23).

✉ Midan Tahrir ☎ 02-575 4319 ⏰ Sat–Thu 9–4:45, Fri 9–11:15, 1:30–4 💷 Moderate; mummies expensive–very expensive

Mathaf el-Mummia (Mummification Museum)

This modern museum explains the process of mummification, which played such an important role in ancient Egyptian funerary rituals. Mummies of both animals and humans are well displayed, as well as the instruments used, ➤ 68.

✉ On the East Bank Corniche, Luxor ⏰ 9–1, 4–9 in winter, 5–10PM in summer

Mathaf el-Watr (Railway Museum)

A fascinating automated display of vintage trains, including Khedive Ismail's private train.

✉ Next to Ramses Station,

Sharia Ramses ☎ 02-763 793
🕐 Tue–Sun 8:30–1. Closed
Mon 💷 Cheap

Mathaf el-Zira'a
(Agricultural Museum)

The oldest agricultural
museum in the world with a
large collection of stuffed
animals and lively, life-size
reproductions of Egyptian
village life. The large garden
has a huge variety of trees.

✉ Next to 6 October Bridge
and the Ministry of Agriculture,
Dokki ☎ 02-702 933/360 8682
🕐 Tue–Sun 9–1:30. Closed
Mon 💷 Cheap

Rowing

The excursion to the Faiyum
and its lake is usually much
appreciated by children. The
countryside is green and full
of animals, most restaurants
on the lake have a
playground, and children can
work off their energy by
rowing beautiful boats on
Lake Qarun (available all
along the shore). ➤ 46.
✉ 100km southwest of Cairo

Theme Parks

Aqua Park

Water-based theme park
with water slides, swimming
pool and an artificial
waterfall.
✉ Misr Isma'ilia Road, Km 6,
Cairo ☎ 02-477 0099 🕐
Daily 💷 Expensive

Cairo Land

A large theme park with
fairground-type rides,
including a water ride. Cairo
Land's Acropolis theatre, a
disco by night, hosts an
afternoon puppet show with
singing and dancing aimed at
younger children.
✉ 1 Sharia Salah Salem, Cairo

☎ 02-364 5251/364 0430
🕐 Daily 💷 Expensive

Dream Park

Part of Dreamland, a huge
leisure complex near the
pyramids with apartments,
shopping malls, clubs and a
golf course, Dream Park has
a number of foreign-made
rides that will get the
adrenalin pumping. The
evocative names are a good
clue to what awaits you – try
Star Spinner, Top Spin, Spill
Water and the Condor. There
are also gentler rides, such
as a monorail train, and
bumper cars and go-karts.
✉ Oasis Road, nr 6th of
October City, Giza ☎ 011-
400561 🕐 Daily 9–midnight
💷 Expensive

Dr Ragab's Pharaonic
Village

A 2-hour guided tour by boat,
quite kitsch but fun, through
the Canal of Mythology,
taking in scenes of ancient
Egyptian rural life, and
ending at a temple with a
sacred lake. Possibility of
dressing like a pharaoh and
posing for a picture. There is
also a restaurant, café and
small playground.
✉ Jacob's Island, Sakiet Miky,
Giza, Cairo ☎ 02-571 8675
🕐 Daily 9–5 (winter), 9–9
(summer) 💷 Expensive

Zoos

Guineenat el-Samak (Fish
Garden)

About 200 displays of
tropical fish set into several
grottoes and a labyrinth of
little alleys which are great
fun for children to explore.
✉ Galabaya Park, Sharia
Hassan Sabri, Zamalek 🕐
Daily 8:30–3 💷 Cheap

Baby Gear

In most tourist centres it is
no problem finding the
baby essentials.
Pharmacies and better
groceries sell powdered
milk and jars of puréed
food. Be warned that
nappies made in Egypt are
not as efficient as those
sold in Europe, and even
though imported varieties
are readily available it may
be useful to take enough
with you for night use.
Sunblock for children is
often but not always
available, and most
necessary at all times.
Bring your own armbands
and inflatable rings for
the sea and pools, as
well as rubber shoes to
protect against corals in
the Red Sea.

Nightclubs & Discos

Disco Etiquette
Some nightclubs in five-star hotels will accept only members and hotel residents on busy evenings. Elsewhere, single men may be refused in favour of couples or mixed groups. Some places will refuse entry to single women, while others will let them in for free. Egyptians usually dress up to go out, so leave the shorts at home, even on hot nights.

The best belly dancers dance at the nightclubs of five-star hotels. There is usually an early performance with dinner at 8–9PM, but most Egyptians and Arabs wait for the late show, which can happen anytime between 1 and 3AM. For a rougher, more popular belly dance show head for one of the Downtown nightclubs around Ezbekiya: there, as it gets later and more money gets thrown at the girls, so the best dancers take to the floor. Do not be offended if you are seated at the back of the hall, as foreigners are not expected to know the art of throwing money on stage.

Cairo
Africana
African disco with a cool atmosphere, good music (African and Egyptian) and lively dancing. Easier environment for women who like to dance on their own.
✉ **Sharia el-Ahram, Giza**
🕙 **9PM–early morning**

Cairo Jazz Club
Although in an unlikely place, the Cairo Jazz Club hosts regular live jazz sessions from foreign and Egyptian musicians. Great atmosphere.
✉ **197, 26th of July Street, beside the Zamalek Bridge, Aguza** ☎ **02-345 9939**
🕙 **7PM–early morning**

Cairo Land Entertainment Centre
Lively venue with two restaurants and the Crazy House Disco with British DJs, fog machine and three sprung dance floors. Popular

with a young, well-heeled Cairene crowd. The Anchovy's Bar also has a disco with 1950s–70s dance music.
✉ **1 Sharia Salah Salem, Abbaseya** ☎ **02-366 1082**

Exit
Funky club, often with African music, and a joyful atmosphere.
✉ **Atlas Hotel, 2 Sharia Mohamed Roushdy, off Midan Opera, Downtown** ☎ **02-391 8127**

Jackie's Joint
Up-market club with British DJs and laser shows, popular with wealthy slightly older (30 plus) Cairenes and foreigners.
✉ **Nile Hilton Hotel, Midan Tahrir, Downtown** ☎ **02-578 0444**

Palmyra
In an authentic 1950s hall, the *madame* with monocle will lead you to your seats and encourage you to drink alcohol while always keeping an eye that the Gulf Arabs do not overdo it with the plump belly dancers.
Recommended if you want something a little bit different.
✉ **Alley off 26th July Street, Ezbekiya**

Tamango
Popular club with young Egyptians and expatriates; it plays good Western dance music mixed with the occasional Egyptian pop hit, the cue for all the Egyptians start to belly dancing.
✉ **Atlas Hotel, Sharia Gama'at el-Duwal el-Arabiya, Mohandiseen** ☎ **02-346 4175**
🕙 **10PM–4AM**

Cinema & Theatre

Cinema

Film and theatre listings appear in the daily *Egyptian Gazette*, the *Egyptian Mail* on Sunday, the weekly *al-Ahram*, *Cairo Times* and the monthly *Insight* and *Egypt Today* magazines. Arabic films are rarely subtitled but quite a few cinemas (main ones listed below) offer English films with or without Arabic subtitles. Foreign film programmes usually change on Wednesday, local ones on Monday.

Cairo

Metro
✉ **35 Sharia Talaat Harb, Downtown** ☎ **02-393 7566**

MGM
✉ **4th floor Maadi Grand Mall** ☎ **02-352 3066**

New Odeon
✉ **Cairo Sheraton, Sharia el-Galaa, Giza** ☎ **02-360 6061**

Ramses Hilton I & II
✉ **7th floor of hotel's annex shopping mall, Corniche el-Nil** ☎ **02-777 444**

Renaissance
✉ **World Trade Centre, 1191 Corniche el-Nil, Boulaq** ☎ **02-580 4039**

Theatre

Cairo
Cairo Opera House
The main hall has 1,200 seats for Egyptian and prestigious international ballet, opera and theatre performances. The smaller hall can hold 500. There is also an open-air theatre. Advance booking is recommended. Men should wear jacket and tie for all performances (except for some in the open-air theatre).
✉ **Gezira Exhibition Grounds, Gezira** ☎ **02-342 0598**

Centre Français de Culture et de Cooperation
Daily French films, new release or repertoire, French or Egyptian plays, bands and good exhibitions.
✉ **1 Sharia Madrasset el-Huquq el-Firensiya, Mounira** ☎ **02-355 3725**

Wallace Theatre
Excellent theatre for Western-style theatre performances and regular concerts.
✉ **American University in Cairo, Sharia Kasr el-Aini, Downtown** ☎ **02-357 5436** 🕐 **Oct–May**

Alexandria
Museum of Fine Arts
Besides the art collection, the museum also organises many concerts and has a film club showing both Arabic and foreign films.
✉ **18 Sharia Menasce, Moharram Bay** ☎ **03-493 6616** 🕐 **Wed 6:30–8:30PM. Closed Fri**

Sayed Darwish Theatre
The old opera house presents opera, theatre and ballet.
✉ **22 Sharia Fouad, opposite Cinema Royale** ☎ **03-482 5106**

Aswan
Aswan Cultural Centre
Daily performances of a folkloric programme including Egyptian and Nubian dance.
✉ **117 Corniche el-Nil** ☎ **097-323 344** 🕐 **Daily at 9:30PM. Closed Fri**

Whirling Dervishes
The Mawlawiyya are the Egyptian branch of the Sufi sect founded in the 13th century in Konya (Turkey), known as the Whirling Dervishes. A good tourist show of these whirling dervishes is staged at the el-Ghuri Cultural Centre in the el-Ghuri Palace (► 35), Sharia el-Azhar, just next to the footbridge. The performances, on Wednesday and Friday at 8PM (check for exact timings ☎ 02-510 0823) are free. Alternatively you can contact the American-run Community Services Association in Maadi (☎ 02-350 5284/376 8232) for details of organised excursions to see the Whirling Dervishes.

Sports

Cairo Hash House Harriers

The Hash House Harriers meet every Friday, two hours before sunset, to jog, walk or run at different locations near Cairo. For information call Bob Williams ☎ 02-348 2658 or Martin Roche ☎ 02-375 2711. The Delta Hash House Harriers organise runs and walks around Alexandria for everyone, every Friday at 2PM from September to June, starting from the Centro de Portugal, Sharia Kafr Abduh in Roushdi. Call Nigel Moore ☎ 03-542 7054 for details.

Cycling

The Cairo Cyclists meet each Friday at 7AM at the front gate of the Cairo American College, 1 Midan Digla, Maadi for a day's cycling. Two groups of mountain bikes and racing bikes also meet on Saturday at 7AM. The club also organises long-distance events for more serious cyclists and can provide information for everyone interested in cycling.
☎ **R Beck 02-350 6647 or E Chrosswhite 02-352 6310.**

Desert Driving

Heading off into remote areas of the desert is becoming increasingly popular, but still takes serious planning, reliable equipment and an experienced guide. Some of the best tour guides include:

Amr Shannon

An artist, who has been leading small groups through Egypt's deserts for more than 20 years
☎ **02-518 6130**

Samir Lama

King of the Western Desert tour guides, who organises several long-range desert expeditions each year into the far southwest of Egypt and into Sudan for small groups of six to eight people. He can be reached in Germany at:
☎ **0049 69 447 897, fax 0049 69 499 0767**

Badawiya

Arrange highly recommended treks throughout the Western Desert and other areas of Egypt.
☎ **02-345 8524**

Abanoub Travel

Run by Dr Rabia, a doctor who fell in love with Sinai and has been leading tours by jeep or camel there ever since.
☎ **062-520 201, fax 062-520 20**

Fishing

Fishing is forbidden off the Sinai shores, but allowed elsewhere in the Red Sea, on the Mediterranean and c the Nile. Boats and guides can be rented in Alexandria and Hurghada. More information is available from The Shooting Club in Cairo ☎ 02-337 3337.
People from all over the world come to Lake Nasser (► 12–13) to fish for elusiv tiger-fish, or Nile perch, one of the biggest freshwater fish in the world, which can weigh more than 100kg.

Aswan

El-Bohayrat Orascom

Has been organising 1- or 2 week fishing safaris with very experienced guides for several years
✉ **PO Box 190, Aswan ☎ 8 fax 097-311 011.**

Gliding

For the best view over Cair and the pyramids, try a gliding excursion, often available on Thursday and Friday from the Egyptian Aviation Society at Imbaba Airfield, west of Cairo.

Golf

Equipment can be rented b golf has become a fashionable sport and courses are very busy.

Dreamland Golf Course

18 holes
✉ **Dreamland, near 6th of October City ☎ 011-400 577**

Gezira Sporting Club
18 holes
✉ Gezira ☎ 02-341 5270/340 5000

Horse-racing

Horse-racing takes place on Saturdays and Sundays from November to May, starting at 1PM, at the Hippodrome Course, Heliopolis in Cairo or at the Smouha Race Course in Alexandria. Horse-races also take place on weekends at the Gezira Club ✉ Saraya el-Gezira ☎ 02-341 5270

Horse Riding

It makes for a fun day out to go by horse from Giza to Saqqara, riding between the villages and the desert, skirting around the pyramids. There are some good stables in the village of Nezlet es-Semaan, near the Sphinx in Giza, where riding lessons are also available (▶ 110). The Saqqara Country Club has wonderful stables and riding facilities (temporary memberships are available).
✉ Saqqara Rd to Abu el-Nomros ☎ 02-384 6115, fax 02-385 0577

Luxor

The Arabian Horse Stable
Has both horses and camels available by the hour for exploring the antiquities or to ride along the Nile.
✉ Behind the Mobil Oil petrol station on the West Bank ☎ 95-310 024

Sharm el-Sheikh

The Fayrouz Hilton
Organises horse trips into the Sinai desert.
☎ 062-600 136, fax 062-601 040

Scuba Diving

All diving centres offer equipment rental and organise boat excursions and diving courses. The main Red Sea resorts (▶ 89) all have shops where you can buy your own snorkelling and diving equipment. The British Sub Aqua Club ☎ 02-331 3500 meets every other Tuesday at the British Embassy for dive-related fun and divers of all nationalities are welcome to join their excellent monthly dive trips to the Red Sea and free training courses. BSAC certification is internationally recognised.

Diving Centres

Dahab
Nesima Diving Centre
✉ Nesima Hotel ☎ 062-640 320/1

Sinai Dive Club
☎ 062-640 465

Hurghada
Aquanaut
✉ Shedwan Golden Beach Hotel ☎ 065-549 891

Barakuda Diving Centre
✉ Giftun Village ☎ 065-442 665 (or Hurghada Marriott Beach Resort ☎ 065-446 950)

Easy Diver Diving Centre
✉ Three Corners Village ☎ 065-548 816

Nuweiba
Aquasport Dive & Watersports Centre
✉ Nuweiba Hilton Coral Resort ☎ 062-520 329

Quseir
Ocean Red Dive Club
✉ Fanadir ☎ 065-439 260

Sub Aqua Dive Centre
✉ Utopia Beach ☎ 065-430 213

Sharm el-Sheikh
Aquamarine Diving Centre
✉ Naama Bay ☎ 062-660 276

Red Sea Diving Club
✉ Naama Bay ☎ 062-660 343

Red Sea Diving College
✉ Naama Bay ☎ 062-660 145

Soccer Crazy
Egyptians are mad about football and when Egypt or one of the local teams plays the streets are empty and silent. From September to May there are football matches every Friday at 3PM and Sunday afternoon. Cairo has two popular teams, Ahli and Zamalek, and taxi drivers often judge your character upon which team you support.

What's On When

Ramadan

During the month of Ramadan, most Muslim Egyptians abstain from drinking, eating, smoking and other pleasures from sunrise to sunset. Businesses work more or less part time and the traffic becomes absolutely frantic in the hour before sunset, as everyone tries to get home to break the fast. In the evening families go to the area around el-Husayn Mosque in Cairo for amusement, tea and a waterpipe. Bars, if open at all, don't serve alcohol to Egyptians, not even to Copts, and it is advisable to take your passport for this reason.

Islamic Festivals

The Islamic calendar is based on a lunar cycle of 12 months of 29 or 30 days, so the Muslim year is 11 days shorter than the Western or Gregorian calendar. This makes it difficult to give exact dates for Muslim festivals. To be sure, check with the Egyptian Tourist Authority.
Ras el-Am (Islamic New Year): first of the month of Muharram
Aid el-Fitr: end of Ramadan
Aid el-Adha (Bayram): holiday when sheep are slaughtered to commemorate Abraham's sacrifice

Moulids

Moulids or celebrations of saints' days take place throughout the year and throughout Egypt. The Moulid el-Nabi (Birthday of the Prophet) is celebrated all over the country, especially near the el-Husayn Mosque (➤ 43) in Cairo. The more important *moulids* such as el-Husayn and Sayyida Zeinab in Cairo, Sayyid el-Badawi in Tanta and Abu el-Haggag in Luxor attract thousands and sometimes millions of believers from all over Egypt and the Islamic world. There are also a few Coptic *moulids* and one Jewish *moulid*.

January
• 7th Jan: Coptic Christmas after 43 days of abstaining from animal products
• end of Jan-beginning Feb: Cairo International Book Fair ☎ 02-575 4069

February
• International Fishing Competition, Hurghada ☎

02-395 3953
• 22 Feb: Dawn rays of the sun reach the sanctuary at Abu Simbel temple

March/April
• Coptic Easter, usually celebrated one week after Western Easter
• Sham el-Nessim: public holiday the Monday after Coptic Easter, dating from pharaonic times, celebrating the onset of spring.

May
• Arab horse festival in el-Sharkia ☎ 055-348 643

August
• Folkloric Art Festival, Ismailiya ☎ 02-354 7818

September
• International Festival for Experimental Theatre, Cairo ☎ 02-516 1422
• Alexandria International Film Festival ☎ 03-574 11.

October
• After the cotton harvest, *moulid* of Sayyid el-Badawi Tanta
• International Egypt Rally (Siag Travel ☎ 02-385 6022)
• 22 Oct: Dawn rays of the sun reach the sanctuary at Abu Simbel temple

November
• International Fishing Competition in Sharm el-Sheikh ☎ 02-395 3953
• 4th Nov: Luxor Festival (dance and music)

December
• Cairo International Film Festival ☎ 02-516 1422
• International Nile Regatta Festival, Cairo and Luxor ☎ 02-393 4350

Practical Matters

Above: *many medicines are
available without prescription*
Right: *welcoming sign in
Cairo's Ramses Square*

TIME DIFFERENCES

GMT	Egypt	Germany	USA (NY)	Netherlands	Spai
→	→	→	←	→	→
12 noon	2PM	1PM	7AM	1PM	1PM

BEFORE YOU GO

WHAT YOU NEED

	UK	Germany	USA	Netherlands
● Required				
○ Suggested				
▲ Not required				
Passport	●	●	●	●
Visa (tourist visa available on arrival)	●	●	●	●
Onward or Return Ticket	▲	▲	▲	▲
Health Inoculations (polio, tetanus, hepatitis)	○	○	○	○
Health Documentation (► 123, Health)	▲	▲	▲	▲
Travel Insurance	○	○	○	○
Driving Licence (International)	●	●	●	●
Car Insurance Certificate (if own car)	●	●	●	●
Car Registration Document (if own car)	●	●	●	●

WHEN TO GO

Cairo

| ▬▬▬▬ | High season |
| ▭▭▭▭ | Low season |

18°C	21°C	23°C	27°C	32°C	34°C	35°C	35°C	32°C	30°C	23°C	18°
JAN	FEB	MAR	APR	MAY	JUN	JUL	AUG	SEP	OCT	NOV	DE

 Sun   Sunshine/Showers

TOURIST OFFICES

In the UK
Egyptian State Tourist
Office
Egyptian House
170 Piccadilly
London W1V 9DD
☎ 020-7493 5282
Fax 020-7408 0295

In the USA
Egyptian Tourist Authority
8383 Wilshire Boulevard
Suite 215, Beverly Hills,
Los Angeles
CA90211
☎ 213-653 8815
Fax 213-653 8961

630 Fifth Avenue
Suite 1706
New York NY10111
☎ 0212-332 2570
Fax 0212-956 6439

POLICE	122
TOURIST POLICE	126
FIRE	180
AMBULANCE	123
ANGLO-AMERICAN HOSPITAL IN CAIRO	02-341 8630

WHEN YOU ARE THERE

ARRIVING

The national airline, EgyptAir, operates flights from most European capitals and the US to Cairo, and a few to Luxor. Charter holidays are available to Luxor, Hurghada and Sinai. The easiest way into town is by limousine (pre-paid in the arrivals hall, fixed prices).

Cairo International Airport Journey times
Distance to city centre

25 kilometres

🚈	N/A
🚌	1 hour
🚗	35–45 minutes

Luxor International Airport Journey times
Distance to city centre

7 kilometres

🚈	N/A
🚌	N/A
🚗	15 minutes

MONEY

The Egyptian pound (LE, *guineh* in Arabic) is divided into 100 piastres (PT, *irsh* in Arabic). There are notes for 25 and 50 piastres and 1, 2, 10, 20, 50, and 100 pounds, coins of 5, 10 piastres. Travellers' cheques, preferably in US$, can be changed in all banks and exchange bureaux (transaction charge). Credit cards are widely accepted at banks, hotels and up-market restaurants, but it is wise to check first. More and more five-star hotels and banks in tourist resorts have automatic cash dispensing machines.

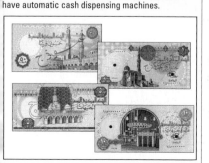

TIME

Egypt stays two hours ahead of GMT most of the year, except during summer time (beginning of May to beginning of October), when it is three hours ahead. Time is a looser concept in Egypt than in Europe: five minutes can mean a few hours, and tomorrow can easily mean next week.

CUSTOMS

→ YES

Declare video cameras and computers on a D-form on arrival, and show on departure. In case of theft report to the police or pay 100 per cent duty.
Alcohol: 1l of liquor, 2l of wine
Cigarettes: 200 *or*
Cigars: 50 *or*
Tobacco: 250g
Perfume: 1l *or*
Toilet water: 1l

In Luxor and Cairo airports there are duty free shops where you can buy another two litres of alcohol on arrival.

— NO

Drugs, firearms (obtain a permit for hunting guns through your travel agent). It is forbidden to export genuine Egyptian antiques from Egypt.

			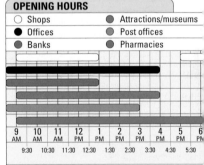	
UK	**Germany**	**Netherlands**	**Spain**	**US**
C2-354 0850	02-341 0015	02-340 1936	02-340 6397	02-355 7371

WHEN YOU ARE THERE

TOURIST OFFICES

Alexandria
- Ramleh Station
  Sharia Saad Zaghloul
  ☎ 03-480 7611
- Misr Railway Station
  ☎ 03-492 5985

Aswan
- Shopping arcade on
  northern end of Corniche
  el-Nil
  ☎ 097-323 297
- Railway station
  ☎ 097-312 811

Cairo
- 5 Sharia Adly, Downtown
  ☎ 02-391 3454
- Giza Pyramids
  ☎ 02-383 0259
- Ramses Railway Station
  ☎ 02-579 0767

El Faiyum
- Governate Building
  Sharia Gumhurriya
  ☎ 084-332 296

Hurghada
- Sharia Bank Misr, beyond
  the Sheraton
  ☎ 065-446 513

Luxor
- Corniche el-Nil
  ☎ 095-373 294
- Luxor Airport
  ☎ 095-373 2215

Port Said
- Sharia Filastine
  ☎ 066-235 289

- **Sharm el-Sheikh**
  Naama Bay
  ☎ 062-660 600

120

NATIONAL HOLIDAYS

J	F	M	A	M	J	J	A	S	O	N	D
1			2	1		1			2		1

1 Jan	New Year's Day
April	Sham el-Nessim
25 Apr	Liberation Day
1 May	Labour Day
23 Jul	Revolution Day
6 Oct	Armed Forces Day
23 Oct	Suez Day
23 Dec	Victory Day

In addition, Egypt observes the traditional feast days
of the Muslim Year and the month of fasting,
Ramadan (➤ 116). The dates of these follow the luna
calendar and therefore move backwards by 11 days
year.

OPENING HOURS

○ Shops	● Attractions/museums
● Offices	● Post offices
● Banks	● Pharmacies

9 AM	10 AM	11 AM	12 PM	1 PM	2 PM	3 PM	4 PM	5 PM	6 PM
9:30	10:30	11:30	12:30	1:30	2:30	3:30	4:30	5:30	

All times given may vary. In tourist areas shops tend
to remain open all day until late at night, especially in
high season. In Ramadan everything tends to open a
least an hour later and close an hour or two earlier,
but shops and some offices reopen 8–10PM. Banks in
tourist areas often stay open all day, until late at
night. Banks at Cairo Airport and Marriott and Nile
Hilton hotels in Cairo are open 24 hours. Museums
and monuments close on Friday for prayers 11–1.
Post Offices are open from Saturday until Thursday.
Pharmacies are often open until 9PM or later.

DRIVE ON THE
RIGHT

TOILETS
BASIC

Use hotels and
restaurants

PUBLIC TRANSPORT

 Internal Flights EgyptAir flies daily from Cairo to most of Egypt's main cities, and Air Sinai flies from Cairo to Hurghada, Sinai and Tel Aviv. Both can be booked through EgyptAir offices (☎ 02-574 7322). The private airline Orascom (☎ 02-301 5632) flies from Cairo and Luxor to el-Gouna.

 Trains The Egyptian State Railway services the Nile Valley, Alexandria, Suez, Port Said and Mersa Matruh. A new line operates from Safaga to Qena, Kharga and Baris. Buy tickets in advance. Wagon-Lits operate a sleeper train from Cairo to Luxor and Aswan, and fast trains to Alexandria. Book in advance from Ramses Station in Cairo (☎ 02-574 9474).

 Buses Buses run from Cairo to most cities in Egypt. Tickets for air-conditioned buses should be booked in advance. Superjet and Golden Rocket operate fast buses to Alexandria (3 hours) and Mersa Matruh from the Abdel Muneem terminal near the Ramses Hilton. Buses for Sinai leave from the Sinai terminal at Abbasiya, and buses for the oases leave from the dusty el-Azhar terminal near Midan Ataba. The Upper-Egyptian Bus Company runs buses to Luxor and Aswan from Midan Ahmed Helmi or 45 Sharia el-Azhar (☎ 02-260 9304).

 Urban Transport Cairo's buses are usually packed to the roof and women are often hassled, so it is advisable to use taxis (► below), which are cheap and more comfortable. The metro is clean and easy to use, especially from Downtown Cairo to Coptic Cairo or Heliopolis.

CAR RENTAL

 Rent a car with a driver. After recent terrorist attacks it is almost impossible to drive anywhere in Egypt without the protection of an armed convoy. You could be asked for your papers at road-blocks and may have to turn back.

TAXIS

 Collective service taxis are usually faster than buses and charge similar rates to bus fares. They usually operate from near bus stations and leave as soon as they have six or seven passengers on board.

DRIVING

 Speed limits on motorways:
120kph

 Speed limits on main roads:
90kph

 Speed limits in urban centres:
50kph

Avoid driving in the dark outside the city as some drivers do not use their lights or switch them on at the last minute, blinding you. Just after sunset people walk their animals home and there is general chaos on rural roads.

 Not compulsory. Only new cars have seatbelts.

 There are many petrol (benzene) stations in the main towns, but fewer out in the countryside. Petrol stations are serviced, not self-serve. Always fill your tank to the limit, and clean the oil filter regularly, as dust and impurities in the petrol tend to clog up the engine. Larger petrol stations are often open until late at night. Petrol is cheaper than in Europe and US.

 Egyptian car mechanics are often masters of invention and can usually be relied upon to fix a broken down car. There are also usually people at hand to help you push your car to the next garage or to the side of the road. Most garages stock a good range of spare parts.

A ruler graphic showing centimetres (0–8) and inches (0–3) scales.

PERSONAL SAFETY

Petty crime remains rare in Egypt but like everywhere else you should watch your belongings in busy tourist areas and on full buses.

- Leave money and valuables in the hotel safe. Carry only what you need.
- There is a crackdown on drugs, with fines for possession, and life imprisonment or hanging for anyone convicted of dealing or smuggling.
- Foreigners travelling between cities usually have to move in a police-protected convoy. There are roadblocks in the main cities at night.

Tourist Police assistance:
☎ 126

Safety in Middle Egypt
The area around Asyut, Dairut and Mallawi has long been a stronghold for Islamic fundamentalists. Since the early 1990s they have targetted foreigners in an attempt to destabilise the country, which depends on tourism. Their campaign of attacks against trains, cruise boats and tourist buses culminated in the attack in 1997 at Deir el-Bahri in Luxor, in which 58 foreigners and 10 Egyptians were killed. In spite of a significant tight-ening of security, at the time of writing it is still advisable to avoid this area.

ELECTRICITY

The power supply in Egypt is 220 volts. Sockets take two-round-pin plugs. British visitors will need an adaptor, US visitors a voltage transformer.

TELEPHONES

Local calls can be made from coin-operated phone boxes, hotels and kiosks. International calls can be made from Telephone and Telegraph (TT) offices. The main branches, at Midan el-Tahrir and at 8 Sharia Adly, are open 24 hours, while other branches are open 7AM–10PM daily. Look for the orange direct-dial telephones which take phone cards that are on sale there. Otherwise, go through an operator, who will charge you a minimum 3 minutes for opening the line. Calls are cheapest between 8PM and 8AM.

International Dialling Codes

From Egypt to:	
UK:	00 44
Germany:	00 49
USA	00 1
Netherlands:	00 31
Spain:	00 34

POST

Stamps can bought at post offices, souvenir shops and hotel newsagents. Airmail letters take about a week to arrive in Europe, a little longer for the USA and Australia. Post your letters in your hotel or use a post office; avoid street letterboxes. Cairo's main post office (open 24 hours) is on Midan el-Ataba.

TIPS/GRATUITIES

Yes ✓ No ✗		
Restaurants (service not included)	✓	8–10%
Restaurants (service included)	✓	change
Cafés/bars	✓	10%
Taxis (negotiate the price first)	✓	5–10%
Museum and site guides	✓	LE2–5
Chambermaids	✓	LE5–10
Porters	✓	LE5–10
Car Parking	✓	LE1–2
Toilets	✓	LE1

PHOTOGRAPHY
What to photograph: everything (exceptions below) – the light in Egypt is wonderful.
What not to photograph: bridges, airports, railway stations, government buildings, dams or anything the authorities consider important to their security. Ask permission before photographing people. Most museums sell special tickets for the use of cameras and videos.
Buying film: avoid buying film lying in bright sunlight, check expiry dates.

HEALTH

Insurance
Egypt has well-qualified doctors and good hospitals, particularly in Cairo and Alexandria. Taking out travel insurance which covers medical care is a must. Keep all receipts and medical bills for reimbursement back home.

Dental Services
Have a check-up before leaving home. In an emergency contact your embassy for a list of English-speaking dentists. There are good dentists in Cairo and Alexandria, but make sure you are covered by medical insurance. English-speaking dentist in Cairo: Maher Labib Barsoum, 26th July Street, Downtown ☎ 02-593 2532/591 5069.

Sun Advice
Use a high factor sunscreen or sunblock, cover up with light cotton clothes, wear sun glasses and a hat when out in the sun. Coffee and alcohol are dehydrating; instead drink plenty of water.

Drugs
Pharmacists (*Saydaliya* in Arabic) usually speak English and can recommend treatment for minor ailments. A wide range of drugs is available over the counter and they are cheap. Check the expiry date and the leaflet to see if it is what you need. Most main cities or resorts have an all-night pharmacy.

Safe Water
It is reasonably safe to drink tap water in the main cities but it is advisable to buy bottles of mineral water, which are widely available. Drink at least 3l of water a day to avoid dehydration from the heat. Avoid ice cubes in drinks.

CONCESSIONS

Students and Youths
Museums and sights offer a 50 per cent reduction on tickets and there are considerable reductions on rail and airline tickets for students who have an official student card. An ISIC Student Card can be issued at the Egyptian Scientific Centre, 23 Sharia el-Manail, above the National Bank, Roda Island, Cairo (☎ 02-363 7251), or at the Ismailiya House (► 100). You need one passport photo and proof that you are a student.

Senior Citizens
There are no special concessions for senior citizens.

CLOTHING SIZES

USA	UK	Europe	
			All these sizes can be found in Egypt, depending on where the clothes have come from
36	36	46	Suits
38	38	48	Suits
40	40	50	Suits
42	42	52	Suits
44	44	54	Suits
46	46	56	Suits
8	7	41	Shoes
8.5	7.5	42	Shoes
9.5	8.5	43	Shoes
10.5	9.5	44	Shoes
11.5	10.5	45	Shoes
12	11	46	Shoes
14.5	14.5	37	Shirts
15	15	38	Shirts
15.5	15.5	39/40	Shirts
16	16	41	Shirts
16.5	16.5	42	Shirts
17	17	43	Shirts
6	8	34	Dresses
8	10	36	Dresses
10	12	38	Dresses
12	14	40	Dresses
14	16	42	Dresses
16	18	44	Dresses
6	4.5	38	Shoes
6.5	5	38	Shoes
7	5.5	39	Shoes
7.5	6	39	Shoes
8	6.5	40	Shoes
8.5	7	41	Shoes

- Reconfirm your flight two days before departing.
- Arrive at the airport at least two hours before departure time, especially at busy times.
- The duty free shops at Egypt's international airports sell some Egyptian souvenirs, books and postcards and a limited selection of alcohol and perfumes.

WHEN DEPARTING

LANGUAGE

The official language in Egypt is Arabic, but English is widely taught in schools. People are always happy, and proud, to practise their foreign languages, but even if you only speak a few words in Arabic you will generally meet with an enthusiastic response. Egyptians elaborate their greetings to each other, even on the telephone, and their love of language and for joking with words is legendary in the Arab world. The following is a phonetic transliteration from the Arabic script.

hotel	funduq	hot water	mayya sokhna
single/double room	oda single/ dubbel	shower	dush
		bathroom	hammam
one night	layla wahda	air-conditioning	takyeef
I have a reservation	'andi hagz	telephone	telefun
		key	muftah
can I see the room	mumkin ashuf el-oda?	lift	ascenseer
		balcony	balacona
is there ...?	fi...?	towel	futa

bank	bank	Egyptian pound	guineh masri
where is the bank?	feen el-bank?	half a pound	nuss guineh
		piastre	irsh
I want to change...	ayyiz/ayza agghayyar... (male/female)	British pound	guineh sterlini
		post office/mail	bosta/barid
money	floos	cheque	cheque
		how much is...?	bi kaam...?

restaurant	mat'am	mineral water	mayya ma'daniya
bon appetit	bi-l-hana wa-sh-shiffa	menu	cart/menu
bill	el-hisab	milk	halib
breakfast	fitaar	salt and pepper	milh wa filfil
tea	shay	wine red, white	nabit ahmar, abyad
coffee	qahwa		
bread	'aysh	beer	beera

right/left	yimeen/shemaa	when does the bus leave?	al-utubees yisaafir emta?
straight ahead	ala toul		
where is...?	feyn...		
the bus station	mahattat al-utubees	...arrive when?	...yawsal emta?
the train station	mahattat al-atr	Is it far/ near?	da baeed/ urayyib
the airport	el-mataar		
I want a taxi	yyiz/ayza taks	here/ there	hinna/hinnaak

yes/no	aywa, na'am/ la'a	hello (to Copts)	sa'eeda
		goodbye	ma'a salaama
thank you	shukran	welcome	ahlan wa sahlan
you're welcome	'afwan		
please	min fadlak (to a man), min fadlik (to a woman)	no problem	ma feesh mushkila
		that is too much	da kateeer awi
God willing	insjallah		
hello (to Muslims)	as-salaamu 'alaykum	impossible	mish mumkin
		my name is ...	ismee...

Acknowledgements

The Automobile Association wishes to thank the following photographers and libraries for their assistance in the preparation of this book.

JAMES MORRIS/AXIOM 35b, 90; BRUCE COLEMAN COLLECTION 89b; MARY EVANS PICTURE LIBRARY 10/11; PAUL STERRY/NATURE PHOTOGRAPHERS 12b; SPECTRUM COLOUR LIBRARY Front cover (d) man on camel, 6b, 41, 66b.

The remaining photographs are held in the Association's own library (AA PHOTO LIBRARY) and were taken by Rick Strange with the exception of the following: CHRIS COE front cover (a) jewellery, (e) relief; back cover pomegranates , 1, 5a, 5b, 6a, 7a, 7b, 8a, 9a, 10, 11, 12a, 14a, 14b, 15a, 16a, 17a, 17b, 18a, 19a, 19b, 20a, 21a, 22a, 23a, 23b, 23c, 24a, 25a, 26a, 26b, 27b, 34, 36b, 38b, 39b, 40b, 42b, 45b, 46b, 49b, 50, 52b, 54b, 57b, 58b, 62b, 65, 66a, 67, 68a, 69, 70, 71, 72, 73a, 73b, 74a, 75a, 77a, 78a, 79a, 79b, 80a, 81a, 82a, 83a, 83b, 85, 87a, 88a, 89a, 117a, 117b, 122a.

Authors' Acknowledgements

The authors would like to thank the following for their help during the research of this book: Mme Samia Khafaga of the Egyptian State Tourist Office, London; Mr Sabri, Inspector of Antiquities, West Bank, Luxor; Siona Jenkins and Mr Wagdy Soliman of Soliman Travel, London.

Copy editor: Anne Heseltine